AN ACCESS GUIDE FOR SCRIPTURE STUDY

The Gospel According to Matthew

John P. Meier

William H. Sadlier, Inc.
New York   Chicago   Los Angeles

Nihil Obstat:
Myles M. Bourke, S.S.L., S.T.D.
Censor Librorum

Imprimatur:
✠ Joseph T. O'Keefe D.D.
Vicar General,
Archdiocese of New York
September 29, 1982

Library of Congress Catalog Card Number: 82-061456
International Standard Book Number: 0-8215-5932-X

 23456789/ 987654

Published by
William H. Sadlier, Inc.
11 Park Place
New York, New York 10007

Printed and bound in the United States of America

Contents

For the Dickman family:
Norbert, Shelley,
Michael, and Matthew,

for their hospitality, friendship, and love.

"Easy access to sacred Scripture should be provided for all the Christian faithful."

Dogmatic Constitution on Divine Revelation, Vatican II

Preface

The study of Scripture is among the oldest and most traditional religious activities in our Christian heritage. The Gospel of Mark and the Gospel of Luke begin their account of Jesus' public ministry by telling us that he read and preached on the Scriptures in the synagogue in Galilee. It was through their knowledge of the Scriptures that Jesus explained the meaning of his death and resurrection to the two disciples on the way to Emmaus. Readings from the Scriptures have been part of our liturgies since the time of the apostles.

Since the Scriptures are not contemporary works, today's audience needs some guidance to understand fully what the authors are trying to communicate to us about the faith of their communities and the events that generated that great faith. Like most carefully written and thoughtful literature, the books of the Bible have depths of meaning not always apparent to the casual reader. Experience tells us that clear guidance and attentive study can be the key to deeper understanding that will lead to rewarding reflection and prayer.

The *Access Guide* series is designed to help beginning and experienced readers of the sacred Scriptures arrive at a better understanding of the books of the

Bible and a familiarity with their role in the development of faith. Each book has been written by a noted authority on that particular part of the Bible. The language is clear, and the text presented in a highly readable manner.

The general introduction of each study guide acquaints the reader with the background of the particular book of the Bible being studied. It provides information about the biblical author, the historical period in which the book was written, and the nature of the community that was the first audience for the book. The theological themes which summarize the author's message are also discussed, giving the reader an idea of what to look for in considering each section of the book.

A thumbnail sketch of each book of the Bible provides the reader with a basic outline that indicates how the author organized his account of the events in order better to communicate his message. It is interesting to note that, in their original form, the books of the Bible were not divided into chapters and verses. Most had no punctuation or even spaces between the words. The organization of the text, as we know it today, took place at a much later date. Often this organization was done by scholars who failed to appreciate the original organization of the authors' thoughts. The sections of the books are organized in these guides in such a way as to reflect the natural internal flow of the original authors' manuscripts.

Likewise, since the ancient Hebrew, Greek, and Aramaic languages are no longer commonly spoken, there are many variations in the way the Scriptures are translated into English. The preferred translation for this series is the *Good News Bible* because of its readability in contemporary English. The reader may choose another translation or wish to compare translations which vary. Certainly, recognizing differences in the interpretation of the Scriptures will enhance the reader's ability to get more out of each passage.

The *Access Guide* series is designed for both group and individual study. All the information needed to use the study guides is provided. Groups, however, may wish to have a discussion leader and use the edition of the *Access Guide* which contains notes for the discussion leader. It is also encouraged that individual readers and group participants have a complete Bible on hand for reference purposes.

The material in each study guide is arranged into six study sessions. This format will help those in discussion groups plan each session around a specific sequence of the Scripture text and give some direction to the discussions. A group leader may find it more convenient to rearrange the material into a greater or fewer number of sessions.

Each of the six study sessions contains a portion of Scripture and commentary. Questions for discussion and reflection are meant to lead the reader to probe more deeply into the significance of the Scripture for its first audience and for the contemporary Christian. Naturally, a renewed understanding of the Scriptures and a fresh discovery of the riches contained therein will lead to reflection and prayer and be shared with others through discussion and celebration.

General Introduction to Matthew, the Gospel of the New and the Old___

The Place of Matthew in the New Testament and in the Church

Although it was not chronologically written first, Matthew's Gospel has been placed by the Church at the beginning of the New Testament. This is not purely accidental. Being one of the longest of the four Gospels, Matthew is one of the largest single treasuries we have of the life and teachings of Jesus. In fact, it is the third longest book in the New Testament (the Gospel of Luke and the Acts of the Apostles are longer). So many of the sayings, miracles, beatitudes, and prayers of Jesus are known to us precisely in their Matthean forms, since Matthew's beautiful phrasing and sonorous, rolling cadences won his version pride of place in the Church's teaching and liturgy. In the old Roman missal, selections from Matthew far outnumbered the ones from Mark and Luke. This centuries-long exposure mainly to Matthew, although redressed in recent years by the new three-year lectionary, still has its effect on our image of Jesus. In the minds and hearts of the faithful, Matthew still remains "the first Gospel."

In developing his text, Matthew drew upon two main documents used by his Church in preaching, teaching and celebrating liturgy: the Gospel of Mark, written around A.D. 70, and a collection of Jesus' sayings which scholars call the "Q document" (from the German *Quelle*, meaning "source"). Adding a large amount of tradition from his own Church (labeled "M material"), Matthew created the breath-taking blend of narrative we have today.

The Purpose of the Writer and the Nature of the Community

One of the most interesting things about Matthew's Gospel is that Matthew is struggling with many problems similar to those with which the Church is struggling today. Then, as now, the Church was experiencing a basic shift in its existence. Faced with a changing situation, it had to adapt and develop its sacred tradition to meet new times.

Matthew's Church had been stringently Jewish in its origins. In the beginning there was much interest in the Mosaic law and resistance to a mission to the gentiles or non-Jews. But by the time Matthew comes to write his Gospel (between A.D. 80–90, probably at Antioch in Syria), the mother Church in Jerusalem had been destroyed, and the Matthean Church had broken its ties with the Jewish synagogue. Consequently, the Jewish past of the Church is fading, while the Church is faced with an increasing number of gentiles swelling its ranks.

This new situation raises many pastoral problems for Matthew and his Church. How is one to adapt the older, more stringent traditions of a Jewish past to this gentile future? How is one to wean the Church away from strict Jewish observances without letting go of basic morality? What is one to make of a group of "Jews for Jesus" who have willy-nilly turned into a universal Church made up of both Jews and gentiles? And how is one to rethink the person and place of Jesus Christ, who is now clearly seen to be not only the Jewish Messiah but also the king of the gentiles, the Lord of the universe and *the* authoritative teacher of morality to all nations?

Christology (the person and work of Jesus Christ), ecclesiology (the nature and mission of the Church), and morality (the practical behavior of disciples in the Church): these are the concerns which absorb Matthew's Church just as they absorb our Church in the 1980s. Both Churches have experienced the jolt or shift in their basic existence, and must now make sense of it.

Theological and Literary Patterns

To meet the crisis of his Church, Matthew brought together various building blocks to form a new structure. He combined many features from the community's traditions about Jesus' life and teachings into a new, unified version of the stages of God's saving plan for his people in history. Matthew distinguishes three periods within the awesome sweep of God's plan:

1. "All prophets and the law" up until, but not including, John the Baptist (11:13);
2. the public ministry of Jesus, restricted to the territory and the people of Israel (10:5–6; 15:24)—all the narrow, traditional Jewish-Christian statements about the law and a mission only to Israel are made to refer to this limited period;
3. the mission to all peoples (28:16–20)—this new universal mission is made possible by the turning point of history, the death and resurrection of Jesus, seen as one great saving event (27:51–54; 28:2–3).

Many other literary patterns are used within this larger framework. The orderly Matthew loves neat, numerically arranged collections of material: nine beatitudes, six antitheses, three pious practices, nine miracle stories. Matthew will also neatly identify the beginning and the end of a particular section of his Gospel by "sandwiching" the section. That is to say, he will place a short, formula-type statement at the beginning of the section, and repeat the statement at the end of the section, thus providing a crisp and clear framework. "Key words," running throughout a section, underline the main recurring themes, and tie the whole section together (see, for example, the use of the key words "child," "greater," "little," "scandalize," in 18:1–14).

More important, theologically, is Matthew's habit of standing back after he narrates an event, to reflect on its meaning. Then he cites an Old Testament passage (usually from the prophets) which sheds light on the event. This technique has been labeled "formula quotation" or "reflection citation." It is used throughout the Gospel, but it is especially noticeable in the infancy narrative of chapters 1 and 2. The formula quotations as a whole emphasize that Jesus Christ is the fulfillment of all the Old Testament law and prophecies.

Major Theological Themes

The central concern of Matthew is the union of Christ and his Church; this union forms the basis for his presentation of morality. All authoritative moral teaching comes from Christ and is preserved, interpreted, and taught by his Church. The Jesus of Matthew's Gospel is a powerful, exalted, solemn figure; the rough undignified aspects of Mark's portrait are omitted. The titles *Son of God* and *Son of Man* serve in particular to stress Jesus' transcendent status as the revealer, teacher, and judge sent by the Father to fulfill his plan for Israel and the world. But a Messiah would not mean much without a messianic people, and so Matthew highlights the community of disciples, the Church, gathered around the Messiah. Indeed, Matthew alone among the four evangelists uses the word "church" in his Gospel. The Church of Jews and gentiles, and not the Israel of old, has become the true people of God by accepting Jesus and obeying his moral teaching. This moral teaching demands the whole-hearted *doing* (not just speaking) of the Father's will; this is what Matthew calls "justice" or "righteousness." All those who do the will of the Father are the true brothers and sisters of Jesus, and thus sons and daughters of his Father, empowered by the Spirit (28:19). The Church is thus the family of God.

A Thumbnail Sketch of Matthew

Matthew's Gospel is like a massive yet intricate piece of architecture. On one side of the main part of the edifice we have the entrance or prologue, formed by the infancy narrative (chapters 1—2). On the other side we have the grand apse, the climax of the whole Gospel, the death and resurrection (chapters 26—28). Since many themes of the death and resurrection are anticipated in the prologue, the whole Gospel is "sandwiched" together by one grand inclusion. In between, the ministry of Jesus is presented in five parts or "books." Each book is made up of a narrative of the deeds of Jesus (miracles, conflict stories, short sayings and parables), followed by a long discourse which comments on some themes raised by the previous narrative. At the same time, the discourse provides a transition to the next book. An outline of the whole Gospel would look something like this:

The Prologue (Chapters 1—2)

The great themes of the death and resurrection are anticipated in the genealogy of Jesus, the annunciation to Joseph, the adoration of the Magi, the flight into Egypt and the slaughter of the children, the return from Egypt and the settling at Nazareth.

Part One:	**Book One (3:1—7:29)** Jesus begins the proclamation of the kingdom.
	Narrative (3:1—4:25) The beginnings of the ministry: John the Baptist; baptism and temptation of Jesus; call of the first disciples.
	Discourse (5:1—7:29) The Sermon on the Mount: the gift and cost of discipleship.
Part Two:	**Book Two (8:1—11:1)** The mission of Jesus and his disciples blossoms in Galilee through deed and word.
	Narrative (8:1—9:38) A cycle of nine miracle stories, arranged in three "trios" of miracles.
	Discourse (10:1—11:1) The disciples imitate the mission of Jesus in Galilee—and beyond.
Part Three:	**Book Three (11:2—13:53)** Conflict breaks out between Jesus and Israel.
	Narrative (11:2—12:50) Jesus enters into debate with the Jewish leaders in a number of conflict stories.
	Discourse (13:1—53) Jesus withdraws from Israel into the mysterious riddle-speech of parables.
Part Four:	**Book Four (13:54—18:35)** Jesus undertakes the formation of his Church and begins to teach her the necessity of his passion and death.
	Narrative (13:54—17:27) The wandering Jesus prepares for the formation of his Church, with a special prominence given to Peter.
	Discourse (18:1—35) Life together in the Church, the family of God, faced with the problems of scandal and sin.
Part Five:	**Book Five (19:1—25:46)** The Messiah leads his embryonic Church up the road to the cross.
	Narrative (19:1—23:39) Jesus continues the formation of his Church as he struggles with Israel for the last time.

Discourse (Chapters 24—25)

Having spoken judgment on the Jewish leaders, Jesus now speaks of the tribulations of the Church and the final judgment on the whole world.

Part Six:
The Climax (Chapters 26—28)

The new age breaks into the old in the shattering events of the death and resurrection of Jesus. The risen Jesus comes to his Church to complete its foundation and send it out on its universal mission.

Origins and Beginnings ____ Matthew 1:1—4:25

The infancy narrative anticipates many themes that will be taken up in the narrative of the death and resurrection of Jesus. The whole of chapters 1 and 2 could be summed up in three important questions:

1. Who is Jesus (identity)? The answer is given largely by titles.
2. Where does he come from (origin)? The answer is given by the genealogy and place names.
3. Where is he going (destiny)? The answer is given by place names and events foreshadowing the death and resurrection, rejection of Israel, and call of the gentiles.

Genealogy

The genealogy at the beginning of the Gospel (1:1—17) signifies that Jesus is the fulfillment and the goal of all of Israel's history. It is a fulfillment containing both continuity and discontinuity in itself. Matthew stresses that his (artificially ordered) genealogy falls into three sections of fourteen generations each.

The Gospel According to Matthew

The Ancestors of Jesus Christ
(Also Luke 3.23–38)

1 This is the birth record of Jesus Christ, who was a descendant of David, who was a descendant of Abraham.

²Abraham was the father of Isaac; Isaac was the father of Jacob; Jacob was the father of Judah and his brothers. ³Judah was the father of Perez and Zerah (their mother was Tamar); Perez was the father of Hezron; Hezron was the father of Ram; ⁴Ram was the father of Amminadab; Amminadab was the father of Nahshon; Nahshon was the father of Salmon; ⁵Salmon was the father of Boaz (Rahab was his mother); Boaz was the father of Obed (Ruth was his mother); Obed was the father of Jesse; ⁶Jesse was the father of King David.

David was the father of Solomon (his mother had been Uriah's wife); ⁷Solomon was the father of Rehoboam; Rehoboam was the father of Abijah; Abijah was the father of Asa; ⁸Asa was the father of Jehoshaphat; Jehoshaphat was the father of Joram; Joram was the father of Uzziah; ⁹Uzziah was the father of Jotham; Jotham was the father of Ahaz; Ahaz was the father of Hezekiah; ¹⁰Hezekiah was the father of Manasseh; Manasseh was the father of Amon; Amon was the father of Josiah; ¹¹Josiah was the father of Jechoniah and his brothers, at the time when the people of Israel were carried away to Babylon.

¹²After the people were carried away to Babylon: Jechoniah was the father of Shealtiel; Shealtiel was the father of Zerubbabel;

¹³Zerubbabel was the father of Abiud; Abiud was the father of Eliakim; Eliakim was the father of Azor; ¹⁴Azor was the father of Zadok; Zadok was the father of Achim; Achim was the father of Eliud; ¹⁵Eliud was the father of Eleazar; Eleazar was the father of Matthan; Matthan was the father of Jacob; ¹⁶Jacob was the father of Joseph, the husband of Mary, who was the mother of Jesus, called the Messiah.

¹⁷So then, there were fourteen sets of fathers and sons from Abraham to David, and fourteen from David to the time when the people were carried away to Babylon, and fourteen from then to the birth of the Messiah.

Matthew mentions four strange women in the course of the genealogy. Mentioning women in genealogies was rare enough, but at least one would expect that the great matriarchs like Sarah or Rachel would be named. Instead, Matthew mentions Tamar, Rahab, Ruth, and (indirectly) Bathsheba, who was the wife of Uriah before she married David.

All of these women had some unusual marital or sexual relationship. This may be interpreted as an inclusion of sinners and/or gentiles in Jesus' descendancy, to emphasize Jesus' mission to save all humankind. On the other hand, a likely explanation is that Matthew presents them as examples of God using unlikely people to advance his plan of salvation, just as he is about to announce the birth of his Son to a virgin from Nazareth.

The Birth of Jesus Christ
(Also Luke 2.1–7)

¹⁸This was the way that Jesus Christ was born. His mother Mary was engaged to Joseph,

but before they were married she found out that she was going to have a baby by the Holy Spirit. [19]Joseph, to whom she was engaged, was a man who always did what was right; but he did not want to disgrace Mary publicly, so he made plans to break the engagement secretly. [20]While he was thinking about all this, an angel of the Lord appeared to him in a dream and said: "Joseph, descendant of David, do not be afraid to take Mary to be your wife. For it is by the Holy Spirit that she has conceived. [21]She will give birth to a son and you will name him Jesus—for he will save his people from their sins."

[22]Now all this happened in order to make come true what the Lord had said through the prophet: [23]"The virgin will become pregnant and give birth to a son, and he will be called Immanuel" (which means, "God is with us").

[24]So when Joseph woke up he did what the angel of the Lord had told him to do and married Mary. [25]But he had no sexual relations with her before she gave birth to her son. And Joseph named him Jesus.

Jesus Announced

The annunciation to Joseph (1:18–25) is Matthew's equivalent of Luke's annunciation to Mary (Luke 1:26–38). In Matthew 1:23 we have the first "formula quotation," reflecting on the narrative in the light of the Old Testament. The name "Jesus" was a popular derivative of "Joshua" which means "Yahweh helps." Writers of the time had refined the interpretation of the name to be "Yahweh saves," which gives rise to the angel's explanation of 1:21. Immanuel is a kind of "throne-name" for the Messiah. In this title is the fulfillment of God's promise to the patriarchs and the prophets: "I shall be with you." Jesus who will save us from sin, and thus remove the barrier between God and his people, is truly "God with us."

Matthew 1:25 says that Joseph did not have sexual relations with Mary (did not know her) "before" she had given birth to Jesus. The "before" does not imply that there was any change afterward. The text in Matthew which is generally the source of challenge to the tradition of Mary's perpetual virginity is 13:55, where four brothers (not cousins) are mentioned. In both cases, Matthew is less interested in biological relationships than he is in theological perspective.

■ *Reflection*

How does my understanding of the historical Joseph and Mary contribute to my devotion to them today?

Visitors from the East

2 Jesus was born in the town of Bethlehem, in the land of Judea, during the time when Herod was king. Soon afterwards some men who studied the stars came from the east to Jerusalem ²and asked: "Where is the baby born to be the king of the Jews? We saw his star when it came up in the east, and we have come to worship him." ³When King Herod heard about this he was very upset and so was everybody else in Jerusalem. ⁴He called together all the chief priests and the teachers of the Law and asked them, "Where will the Messiah be born?" ⁵"In the town of Bethlehem, in Judea," they answered. "This is what the prophet wrote:

⁶'You, Bethlehem, in the land of Judah,
Are not by any means the least among
the rulers of Judah;

For from you will come a leader
Who will guide my people Israel.' "

⁷So Herod called the visitors from the east to a secret meeting and found out from them the exact time the star had appeared. ⁸Then he sent them to Bethlehem with these instructions: "Go and make a careful search for the child, and when you find him let me know, so that I may go and worship him too." ⁹With this they left, and on their way they saw the star—the same one they had seen in the east—and it went ahead of them until it came and stopped over the place where the child was. ¹⁰How happy they were, what gladness they felt, when they saw the star!

¹¹They went into the house and saw the child with his mother Mary. They knelt down and worshiped him; then they opened their bags and offered him presents: gold, frankincense, and myrrh.

¹²God warned them in a dream not to go back to Herod; so they went back home by another road.

The Escape to Egypt

¹³After they had left, an angel of the Lord appeared in a dream to Joseph and said: "Get up, take the child and his mother and run away to Egypt, and stay there until I tell you to leave. Herod will be looking for the child to kill him." ¹⁴So Joseph got up, took the child and his mother, and left during the night for Egypt, ¹⁵where he stayed until Herod died.

This was done to make come true what the Lord had said through the prophet, "I called my Son out of Egypt."

The Killing of the Children

¹⁶When Herod realized that the visitors from the east had tricked him, he was furious. He gave orders to kill all the boys in Bethlehem and its neighborhood who were two years old and younger—in accordance with what he had learned from the visitors about the time when the star had appeared.

¹⁷In this way what the prophet Jeremiah had said came true:
> ¹⁸"A sound is heard in Ramah,
> The sound of bitter crying and weeping.
> Rachel weeps for her children,
> She weeps and will not be comforted,
> Because they are all dead."

The Return from Egypt

¹⁹After Herod had died, an angel of the Lord appeared in a dream to Joseph, in Egypt, ²⁰and said: "Get up, take the child and his mother, and go back to the country of Israel, because those who tried to kill the child are dead." ²¹So Joseph got up, took the child and his mother, and went back to the country of Israel.

²²When he heard that Archelaus had succeeded his father Herod as king of Judea, Joseph was afraid to settle there. He was given more instructions in a dream, and so went to the province of Galilee ²³and made his home in a town named Nazareth. He did this to make come true what the prophets had said, "He will be called a Nazarene."

The Magi

Historically, the Magi or wise men were members of the priestly caste in Persia, though later the word came to mean anyone who had occult knowledge or power. The word could even connote frauds dabbling in magic or superstition. Matthew uses the Magi to represent the gentiles who, like Balaam in Numbers, chapter 24, bring blessings to Israel rather than a curse. The contrast is made between Herod and the Jewish leadership who reject the king of the Jews, and the gentile astrologers who bow down in worship.

The star announces the birth of Jesus; notice that it does not act as a guide to the precise place of birth until after the Magi leave Jerusalem. The nature of the three gifts probably comes from a combination of Psalm 72:10–15 and Isaiah 60:6. Eventually the number of gifts determined the tradition that there were three Magi.

One of the important themes in Matthew is that Jesus sums up in himself the great events of Israel's sacred history. He, in his own person, is the new Israel. Like Moses, Jesus escapes the slaughter of male children to become the salvation of his people, to rescue them from slavery. In Hosea 11:1, the Lord calls Israel his son. In Matthew Jesus is God's Son, like Israel, called forth from exile in Egypt.

Luke and Matthew seem to have different ideas about what was the original hometown of Joseph and Mary. According to Luke, Joseph and Mary are from Nazareth, and come to Bethlehem for the census. Matthew's Gospel gives the impression that Joseph and Mary were residents of Bethlehem. They went to Nazareth to avoid Archelaus (son of Herod, King of Judea), and in obedience to "instructions in a dream."

The Preaching of John the Baptist
(Also Mark 1.1—8; Luke 3.1—18; John 1.19—28)

3 At that time John the Baptist came and started preaching in the desert of Judea. [2]"Turn away from your sins," he said, "for the Kingdom of heaven is near!" [3]John was the one that the prophet Isaiah was talking about when he said:

> "Someone is shouting in the desert:
> 'Get the Lord's road ready for him,
> Make a straight path for him to
> travel!' "

[4]John's clothes were made of camel's hair; he wore a leather belt around his waist, and ate locusts and wild honey. [5]People came to him from Jerusalem, from the whole province of Judea, and from all the country around the Jordan river. [6]They confessed their sins and he baptized them in the Jordan.

[7]When John saw many Pharisees and Sadducees coming to him to be baptized, he said to them: "You snakes—who told you that you could escape from God's wrath that is about to come? [8]Do the things that will show that you have turned from your sins. [9]And do not think you can excuse yourselves by saying, 'Abraham is our ancestor.' I tell you that God can take these rocks and make descendants for Abraham! [10]The ax is ready to cut the trees at the roots; every tree that does not bear good fruit will be cut down and thrown in the fire. [11]I baptize you with water to show that you have repented; but the one who will come after me will baptize you with the Holy Spirit and fire. He is much greater than I am; I am not good enough even to carry his sandals. [12]He has his winnowing-shovel with him, to thresh out all

the grain; he will gather his wheat into his barn, but burn the chaff in a fire that never goes out!''

John the Baptist

Matthew portrays the appearance of the Baptist in verses 1–6. He associates John with the Christian Church, making him a preacher of stringent moral demands. Thus, Matthew makes repentance, not baptism, the direct object of John's preaching. John's message parallels perfectly Jesus' message in 4:17; Matthew tends to portray John and Jesus as parallel figures. For Matthew, repentance means not a compulsive brooding over the past, nor over particular external actions. Repentance is a change of heart and mind, spilling over into changed behavior. This change of heart is always a response to God's prior action of breaking into our world and setting up his definitive rule (the coming of the kingdom).

Matthew presents John's vehement sermon against the Pharisees and Sadducees. These two groups were actually opposed to each other, but Matthew tends to see all Jewish parties as a united front against Jesus, his disciples—and even the Baptist. John rebukes the religious leaders for imagining that a water ritual, instead of a change of heart and behavior, can rescue them from the fiery judgment to come. The same holds true for baptized Christians. God is not dependent on any blood tie or ritual. He can create candidates for salvation (children of Abraham) out of stones—or, as we see at the end of the Gospel, a holy people out of gentiles.

■ *Reflection*
Do I view my own baptism as a sign of repentance? How has it helped me overcome sin?

The Baptism of Jesus
(Also Mark 1.9–11; Luke 3.21–22)

¹³At that time Jesus went from Galilee to the Jordan, and came to John to be baptized by him. ¹⁴But John tried to make him change his mind. "I ought to be baptized by you," John said, "yet you come to me!" ¹⁵But Jesus answered him, "Let it be this way for now. For in this way we shall do all that God requires." So John agreed.

¹⁶As soon as Jesus was baptized, he came up out of the water. Then heaven was opened to him, and he saw the Spirit of God coming down like a dove and lighting on him. ¹⁷And then a voice said from heaven, "This is my own dear Son, with whom I am well pleased."

The ministry of the Baptist naturally culminates in the baptism of Jesus (3:13–17). The emphasis in this story is not on the baptism itself, but on the revelation of Jesus' messianic dignity even before his baptism. Hence, in Matthew alone does John try to prevent Jesus from taking part in a ritual aimed at sinners. Jesus, however, rejects John's expectations of a judge and punisher of sinners. Jesus chooses to take his stand with the sinner rather than over against the penitent.

The title "Son of God" could arouse pipe dreams of easy glory: the crown without the cross. It is to counter this facile idea of divine sonship that Matthew balances the baptism of Jesus with his temptation (4:1–11), which tests and defines his sonship.

The Temptation of Jesus
(Also Mark 1.12–13; Luke 4.1–13)

4 Then the Spirit led Jesus into the desert to be tempted by the Devil. ²After spending forty days and nights without food, Jesus was hungry. ³The Devil came to him and said, "If you are God's Son, order these stones to turn into bread." ⁴Jesus answered, "The scripture says, 'Man cannot live on bread alone, but on every word that God speaks.'"

⁵Then the Devil took Jesus to the Holy City, set him on the highest point of the Temple, ⁶and said to him, "If you are God's Son, throw yourself down to the ground; for the scripture says,

'God will give orders to his angels
    about you:
They will hold you up with their hands,
So that you will not even hurt your feet
    on the stones.'"

⁷Jesus answered, "But the scripture also says, 'You must not put the Lord your God to the test.'"

⁸Then the Devil took Jesus to a very high mountain and showed him all the kingdoms of the world, in all their greatness. ⁹"All this I will give you," the Devil said, "if you kneel down and worship me." ¹⁰Then Jesus answered, "Go away, Satan! The scripture says, 'Worship the Lord your God and serve only him!'"

¹¹So the Devil left him; and angels came and helped Jesus.

¹²When Jesus heard that John had been put in prison, he went away to Galilee. ¹³He did not settle down in Nazareth, but went and lived in Capernaum, a town by Lake Galilee, in the territory of Zebulun and Naphtali. ¹⁴This was done

to make come true what the prophet Isaiah had said:

> [15]"Land of Zebulun, land of Naphtali,
> In the direction of the sea, on the other side of Jordan,
> Galilee of the Gentiles!
> [16]The people who live in darkness
> Will see a great light!
> On those who live in the dark land of death
> The light will shine!"

[17]From that time Jesus began to preach his message: "Turn away from your sins! The Kingdom of heaven is near!"

Triumph in the Desert

Three times Jesus, the true Son of God, triumphs in the desert just as Israel failed. The three temptations of hunger, presumption, and idolatry are all recorded in Deuteronomy. It is not by accident, then, that each time Jesus rejects Satan's suggestion that Jesus misuse his sonship he does so by quoting Deuteronomy (8:3; 6:16; 6:13). Jesus defines his divine sonship in terms of obedience and trust, tested by suffering.

Matthew sees Jesus' move to Capernaum and his initial act of preaching (4:12–17) as a fulfillment of Isaiah 8:23—9:1. Jesus is the messianic light shed upon Jews living in a land threatened by pagan darkness. "Galilee, land of the Gentiles!" in chapter 4 conjures up the image of a religiously deprived region. But it also points forward to the Gospel's final scene, when the risen Messiah sends forth his disciples from Galilee to all nations, Jews and gentiles alike.

The First Disciples

A kingdom needs subjects; a messiah needs a people. So Jesus' initial proclamation is followed by his first call of disciples (4:18–22). At this point in Matthew's narrative, these four disciples are needed to provide the proper audience for the Sermon on the Mount. The call of Peter, Andrew, James and John stresses the all-powerful Word of the Lord who issues the call, and the immediate, total obedience of the men who are called. These men have had no preparation for Jesus' invasion of their lives. In the midst of their ordinary work they are suddenly claimed for God's work.

Besides the close circle of disciples, there are the larger crowds which "follow" Jesus in less than the full sense of discipleship. These crowds will provide both the remote audience for the Sermon on the Mount and a pool of potential converts (4:23–25).

Jesus' activity on behalf of the crowds is summed up by three key verbs. (1) *Jesus teaches.* Notice the lack of an object here. *What* Jesus teaches will be explained at length in the Sermon on the Mount and the other discourses. Only Jesus teaches in the proper sense during the public ministry. The disciples will be empowered to teach only after the resurrection. (2) *Jesus proclaims* or preaches the good news of the kingdom: God is initiating his complete rule over the world. Matthew betrays his own priorities by putting teaching before proclaiming. He is intent on our moral response to God's action in our lives. (3) *Jesus heals,* for the Word of Jesus is dynamic: it effects what it proclaims. The kingdom which Jesus proclaims is made present in the lives of his audience by his healing Word. The great crowds, attracted by this teaching, proclaiming and healing Word, assemble around the great mount of teaching for Jesus' inaugural sermon.

■ *Reflection*

*Has the Word of Jesus had the same effect on my life
that Matthew describes in the Gospel?*

Jesus Calls Four Fishermen
(Also Mark 1.16–20; Luke 5.1–11)

¹⁸As Jesus walked by Lake Galilee, he saw
two brothers who were fishermen, Simon
(called Peter) and his brother Andrew, catching
fish in the lake with a net. ¹⁹Jesus said to them,
"Come with me and I will teach you to catch
men." ²⁰At once they left their nets and went
with him.

²¹He went on and saw two other brothers,
James and John, the sons of Zebedee. They
were in their boat with their father Zebedee,
getting their nets ready. Jesus called them; ²²at
once they left the boat and their father, and
went with Jesus.

Jesus Teaches, Preaches, and Heals
(Also Luke 6.17–19)

²³Jesus went all over Galilee, teaching in
their synagogues, preaching the Good News of
the Kingdom, and healing people from every
kind of disease and sickness. ²⁴The news about
him spread through the whole country of Syria,
so that people brought him all those who were
sick with all kinds of diseases, and afflicted
with all sorts of troubles: people with demons,
and epileptics, and paralytics—Jesus healed
them all. ²⁵Great crowds followed him from
Galilee and the Ten Towns, from Jerusalem,
Judea, and the land on the other side of the
Jordan.

■ Discussion

1. Considering the many sources Matthew uses to form the basis of his Gospel, what is the relationship between history and the theological outlook of the Gospel writer?

2. What themes found in the infancy narrative relate to the events told later in the Gospel concerning Jesus as teacher, the passion and death, and the resurrection?

3. Based on Matthew's Gospel, what would you say is the relationship between Jesus and John the Baptist?

4. What references to the events of Moses' life and the Exodus are present in Matthew's story of Jesus? Why does Matthew compare Jesus with Moses?

5. What actions of Jesus' ministry give evidence that he is the Messiah, the savior of the world?

■ Prayer and Meditation

"A child is born to us!
    A son is given to us!
    And he will be our ruler.
He will be called, 'Wonderful Counselor,'
    'Mighty God,' 'Eternal Father,'
    'Prince of Peace.' "

Isaiah 9:6

The Sermon on the Mount———Matthew 5:1—8:8

The Sermon on the Mount is the first of the five great discourses which Matthew carefully distributes throughout the public ministry of Jesus. Each discourse is connected with the narrative which precedes it. Matthew has just finished describing the call of the first disciples, who *follow* Jesus. At the end of chapter 4 he mentions the larger crowds which *follow* Jesus from all areas of the Holy Land. The first discourse now explains what following Jesus means to one's moral life.

The Sermon on the Mount has been put together by Matthew from various sources. The sayings, for the most part, go back to Jesus himself, but the order and the structure of the sermon come from Matthew. Up until 6:18, Matthew orders the blocks of material in neat numerical patterns. After 6:18, the connections become looser. The subsequent material might be considered a meditation on the various petitions of the Our Father.

In 5:1, Matthew sets the scene: Jesus goes up the mountain. Mountains are important symbols in Matthew's Gospel. They signify the place of revelation, the place where the Father gives teaching to people. In chapters 5—7, Jesus is revealing the "Law of Discipleship," the code of attitude and conduct for those who wish to follow him, just as Moses was given the covenant between God and Israel on a mountain. In this case, Jesus is the one giving the law instead of receiving it. He is not merely taking the role of a new Moses, but acting as God himself.

The Sermon on the Mount

5 Jesus saw the crowds and went up a hill, where he sat down. His disciples gathered around him, ²and he began to teach them:

> ³"Happy are those who know they are
>   spiritually poor:
>   the Kingdom of heaven belongs to
>   them!
> ⁴"Happy are those who mourn:
>   God will comfort them!
> ⁵"Happy are the meek:
>   they will receive what God has
>   promised!
> ⁶"Happy are those whose greatest
>   desire is to do what God
>   requires:
>   God will satisfy them fully!
> ⁷"Happy are those who show mercy to
>   others:
>   God will show mercy to them!
> ⁸"Happy are the pure in heart:
>   they will see God!
> ⁹"Happy are those who work for peace
>   among men:
>   God will call them his sons!
> ¹⁰"Happy are those who suffer
>   persecution because they do
>   what God requires:
>   the Kingdom of heaven belongs to
>   them!

¹¹"Happy are you when men insult you and mistreat you and tell all kinds of evil lies against you because you are my followers. ¹²Rejoice and be glad, because a great reward is kept for you in heaven. This is how men mistreated the prophets who lived before you."

The Beatitudes

Before there is any statement of fierce demands, Jesus pronounces the nine Beatitudes, the proclamation of the good news of the happiness God offers us. Only those who have heard and believed this happy good news are capable of hearing and acting on Jesus' demands. God's Word and action always precede and make possible our moral response.

The Beatitudes are literally the "happy attitudes," since the word "blessed" in the Beatitudes really means "happy." Jesus is defining what true happiness is, a happiness which comes from God. God becomes the judge of the inner person in each of the Beatitudes. They are spiritually poor, humble; they are pure in heart. Their inner disposition gives rise to action—they mourn, are merciful to others, work for peace. These attitudes and good works are rewarded through God's judgment.

The contrast is with those who use the law as a standard, and observe ritual purity and periods of mourning, who are proud of the appearances of piety and righteousness. The religious leaders insisted on the letter of the law, but did not keep it in spirit. The Hellenistic rulers of the time claimed to be peacemakers and descendants from gods, but were men of violence, and not God's children. The listing of four "passive" Beatitudes followed by five "active" Beatitudes clearly links inner disposition and good works as the signs of the true disciple in Matthew. The followers of Jesus will be perse-cuted (a reference to the members of Matthew's Church), but they will be rewarded for their fidelity to Jesus' teaching.

Salt and Light
(Also Mark 9.50; Luke 14.34–35)

¹³"You are like salt for all mankind. But if salt loses its taste, there is no way to make it salty again. It has become worthless; so it is thrown away and people walk on it.

¹⁴"You are like light for the whole world. A city built on a hill cannot be hid. ¹⁵Nobody lights a lamp to put it under a bowl; instead he puts it on the lamp-stand, where it gives light for everyone in the house. ¹⁶In the same way your light must shine before people, so that they will see the good things you do and give praise to your Father in heaven."

Salt and Light

When Matthew moves to the parables of salt, light and the city in 5:13–16, he emphasizes the personal obligation of the disciples: "*You* are . . . *you* are." We should remember that salt was a precious and vital commodity for the ancient world. Making covenants, preserving food, symbolizing peace, and table fellow-ship—these and many other functions were served by salt. The disciples who will be persecuted are actually the salvation of those who reject them. But they must remain active witnesses to Jesus' teaching in order to keep their place as salt and light and the exalted city. Only they can lose their flavor, and extinguish the light of salvation.

■ Reflection

How can I be "salt" and "light" in my own community?

Teaching About the Law

[17]"Do not think that I have come to do away with the Law of Moses and the teaching of the prophets. I have not come to do away with them, but to give them real meaning. [18]Remember this! As long as heaven and earth last, the least point or the smallest detail of the Law will not be done away with—not until the end of all things. [19]Therefore, whoever disobeys even the smallest of the commandments, and teaches others to do the same, will be least in the Kingdom of heaven. On the other hand, whoever obeys the Law, and teaches others to do the same, will be great in the Kingdom of heaven. [20]I tell you, then, that you will be able to enter the Kingdom of heaven only if you are more faithful than the teachers of the Law and the Pharisees in doing what God requires."

The Law

In 5:17–20, Jesus sets down some basic principles about the Mosaic law and how it relates to himself. Despite all that is to follow in the instructions of 5:21–48, the disciples are not to imagine that Jesus' mission is to wipe out the revelation of God's will in the Old Testament, the law, and the prophets. Rather, Jesus has come to *fulfill* the law and the prophets. Yet in 5:21–48 he goes on to set aside some important elements of the written law.

Matthew 5:18 speaks about not the smallest part of the law passing away. While this seems to contradict the revocation of the law which is to come in the list of instructions, it does express a time limit: "until the end of all things," that is, until all the prophecies about Christ are fulfilled. At first glance this seems to mean the end of the world: "as long as heaven and earth last." But Matthew represents the death-resurrection of Jesus as the great turning point of history, the breaking in of the new age.

Having stated the basic principle about the law, Jesus now gives six concrete examples of what Christian justice involves. These examples are called "antitheses" because of the contrast between two commands. The contrast is underlined by the formula "You have heard . . . but now I tell you." God is the speaker referred to in the phrase "you have heard." In other words, God said, "Do not commit murder," and "Do not commit adultery," and the like. This is why in 5:17–19 Matthew insists that Jesus was *not* going to abolish the whole law.

Teaching About Anger

[21]"You have heard that men were told in the past, 'Do not murder; anyone who commits murder will be brought before the judge.' [22]But now I tell you: whoever is angry with his brother will be brought before the judge; whoever calls his brother 'You good-for-nothing!' will be brought before the Council; and whoever calls his brother a worthless fool will be in danger of going to the fire of hell. [23]So if you are about to offer your gift to God at the altar and there you remember that your brother has something against you, [24]leave your gift there in front of the altar and go at once to make peace with your brother; then come back and offer your gift to God.

²⁵"If a man brings a lawsuit against you and takes you to court, be friendly with him while there is time, before you get to court; once you are there he will turn you over to the judge, who will hand you over to the police, and you will be put in jail. ²⁶There you will stay, I tell you, until you pay the last penny of your fine."

Teaching About Adultery

²⁷"You have heard that it was said, 'Do not commit adultery.' ²⁸But now I tell you: anyone who looks at a woman and wants to possess her is guilty of committing adultery with her in his heart. ²⁹So if your right eye causes you to sin, take it out and throw it away! It is much better for you to lose a part of your body than to have your whole body thrown in hell. ³⁰If your right hand causes you to sin, cut it off and throw it away! It is much better for you to lose one of your limbs than to have your whole body go off to hell."

In the first antithesis (5:21–26), the escalating scale of punishments (trial . . . council . . . fire of hell) probably is meant to mock any hair-splitting casuistry. Verses 23–26 turn to the allied idea of reconciliation after a quarrel.

The second antithesis makes clear that sin takes place first of all in the heart. The harsh teaching and shocking images in verses 29–30 are not to be taken literally. They reinforce the point that sinfulness is not restricted to overt acts, in this case, adultery.

Teaching About Divorce
(Also Matt. 19.9; Mark 10.11–12; Luke 16.18)

[31]"It was also said, 'Anyone who divorces his wife must give her a written notice of divorce.' [32]But now I tell you: if a man divorces his wife, and she has not been unfaithful, then he is guilty of making her commit adultery if she marries again; and the man who marries her also commits adultery."

Teaching About Vows

[33]"You have also heard that men were told in the past, 'Do not break your promise, but do what you have sworn to do before the Lord.' [34]But now I tell you: do not use any vow when you make a promise; do not swear by heaven, because it is God's throne; [35]nor by earth, because it is the resting place for his feet; nor by Jerusalem, because it is the city of the great King. [36]Do not even swear by your head, because you cannot make a single hair white or black. [37]Just say 'Yes' or 'No'—anything else you have to say comes from the Evil One."

Teaching About Revenge
(Also Luke 6.29–30)

[38]"You have heard that it was said, 'An eye for an eye, and a tooth for a tooth.' [39]But now I tell you: do not take revenge on someone who does you wrong. If anyone slaps you on the right cheek, let him slap your left cheek too. [40]And if someone takes you to court to sue you for your shirt, let him have your coat as well. [41]And if one of the occupation troops forces you to carry his pack one mile, carry it another

mile. ⁴²When someone asks you for something, give it to him; when someone wants to borrow something, lend it to him."

Love for Enemies
(Also Luke 6.27–28, 32–36)

⁴³"You have heard that it was said, 'Love your friends, hate your enemies.' ⁴⁴But now I tell you: love your enemies, and pray for those who mistreat you, ⁴⁵so that you will become the sons of your Father in heaven. For he makes his sun to shine on bad and good people alike, and gives rain to those who do right and those who do wrong. ⁴⁶Why should you expect God to reward you, if you love only the people who love you? Even the tax collectors do that! ⁴⁷And if you speak only to your friends, have you done anything out of the ordinary? Even the pagans do that! ⁴⁸You must be perfect—just as your Father in heaven is perfect."

The third antithesis, in verses 31–32, forbids divorce. The special proviso or exception added by Matthew, translated variously as unfaithfulness, immorality, or unchasteness, probably refers to a prohibition of incestuous unions. Accordingly, it really does not water down Jesus' position against divorce. Compare the longer form of Jesus' teaching on divorce in 19:1–12.

The fourth antithesis, in 5:33–37, forbids oaths and vows. Matthew points out that all oaths are objectionable because they imply that man can somehow control what is in God's power. Obviously this prohibition is contrary to both Old Testament and Christian religious practice.

Another example of the stringent nature of Jesus' teaching in Matthew's Gospel is the fifth antithesis (5:38–42) in which Jesus forbids all retaliation, especially by appeal to courts and lawsuits. By so doing, Jesus points out the uniqueness of the kingdom and its justice. Worldly concerns for equality under the law are no longer operative, since the kingdom is a reality for the disciple.

The sixth antithesis, in 5:43–48, commands not only love of neighbor, but also love of enemies. In this way the disciple will mirror the Father's love for all, good and bad, faithful and faithless, again a sign of the kingdom come in the "end time."

Teaching About Charity

6 "Be careful not to perform your religious duties in public so that people will see what you do. If you do these things publicly you will not have any reward from your Father in heaven.

²"So when you give something to a needy person, do not make a big show of it, as the show-offs do in the synagogues and on the streets. They do it so that people will praise them. Remember this! They have already been paid in full. ³But when you help a needy person, do it in such a way that even your closest friend will not know about it, ⁴but it will be a private matter. And your Father, who sees what you do in private, will reward you."

Teaching About Prayer
(Also Luke 11.2—4)

[5]"And when you pray, do not be like the show-offs! They love to stand up and pray in the synagogues and on the street corners so that everybody will see them. Remember this! They have already been paid in full. [6]But when you pray, go to your room and close the door, and pray to your Father, who is unseen. And your Father, who sees what you do in private, will reward you.

[7]"In your prayers do not use a lot of words, as the pagans do, who think that God will hear them because of their long prayers. [8]Do not be like them; your Father already knows what you need before you ask him. [9]This is the way you should pray:

'Our Father in heaven:
May your name be kept holy,
[10]May your Kingdom come,
May your will be done on earth as it is
    in heaven.
[11]Give us today the food we need;
[12]Forgive us the wrongs that we have
    done,
As we forgive the wrongs that others
    have done us.
[13]Do not bring us to hard testing, but
    keep us safe from the Evil One.'

[14]"For if you forgive others the wrongs they have done you, your Father in heaven will also forgive you. [15]But if you do not forgive the wrongs of others, then your Father in heaven will not forgive the wrongs you have done."

44

[16]"And when you fast, do not put on a sad face like the show-offs do. They go around with a hungry look so that everybody will be sure to see that they are fasting. Remember this! They have already been paid in full. [17]When you go without food, wash your face and comb your hair, [18]so that others cannot know that you are fasting—only your Father, who is unseen, will know. And your Father, who sees what you do in private, will reward you."

Prayer

In 6:1–18, Jesus turns to three pious practices esteemed in Judaism: almsgiving, prayer, and fasting. In so doing, Jesus denounces hypocrisy and hypocrites. These people direct their prayer and good works not to God, but to the people around them who may praise them for their goodness. Jesus is not, however, denouncing communal prayer or community action. He is encouraging the proper motivation for prayer, fasting, and almsgiving.

The natural continuation of 6:5–6 would be verses 17–18. But Matthew seizes the opportunity to insert a separate instruction on prayer, which includes the Our Father. We possess the Lord's Prayer in two forms: the well-known version of Matthew, and the less well-known but probably more original form of Luke 11:1–4.

The Our Father is an example of prayer which seeks not to manipulate, but to acknowledge God's power and goodness. The first three petitions, the "thou petitions" are concerned with the triumph of God's cause, not ours. The unspoken agent of the actions is God, not ourselves: *you* hallow your name, *you* make your kingdom come. The three petitions ask for the final coming of the kingdom; they literally request the end of the world.

The three "we petitions" which follow are also to be seen in the light of the kingdom. "Our daily bread" can be interpreted in a eucharistic sense. Forgiveness of others is seen as a necessary condition for God's forgiveness in the kingdom. The test which we beg not to be brought to could refer to the final, fearful clash between good and evil just before the last day: the fierce testing of the elect in the crucible of suffering (see the Book of Revelation of St. John).

Matthew returns to the main three-part teaching on pious practices in 6:16–18. He again stresses the relationship between God and the believer. No reward will be given to those seeking only human recognition.

■ *Reflection*

Why is the Lord's Prayer an important event in the celebration of the Eucharist, and in the Christian's daily life?

Riches in Heaven
(Also Luke 12.33–34)

[19]"Do not save riches here on earth, where moths and rust destroy, and robbers break in and steal. [20]Instead, save riches in heaven, where moths and rust cannot destroy, and robbers cannot break in and steal. [21]For your heart will always be where your riches are."

The Light of the Body
(Also Luke 11.34–36)

[22]"The eyes are like a lamp for the body: if your eyes are clear, your whole body will be full of light; [23]but if your eyes are bad, your

body will be in darkness. So if the light in you turns out to be darkness, how terribly dark it will be!"

God and Possessions
(Also Luke 16.13; 12.22–31)

[24]"No one can be a slave to two masters: he will hate one and love the other; he will be loyal to one and despise the other. You cannot serve both God and money.

[25]"This is why I tell you: do not be worried about the food and drink you need to stay alive, or about clothes for your body. After all, isn't life worth more than food? and isn't the body worth more than clothes? [26]Look at the birds flying around: they do not plant seeds, gather a harvest, and put it in barns; your Father in heaven takes care of them! Aren't you worth much more than birds? [27]Which one of you can live a few years more by worrying about it?

[28]"And why worry about clothes? Look how the wild flowers grow: they do not work or make clothes for themselves. [29]But I tell you that not even Solomon, as rich as he was, had clothes as beautiful as one of these flowers. [30]It is God who clothes the wild grass—grass that is here today, gone tomorrow, burned up in the oven. Will he not be all the more sure to clothe you? How little is your faith! [31]So do not start worrying: 'Where will my food come from? or my drink? or my clothes? ([32]These are the things the heathens are always after.) Your Father in heaven knows that you need all these things. [33]Instead, give first place to his Kingdom and to what he requires, and he will provide you with all these other things. [34]So do not

worry about tomorrow; it will have enough
worries of its own. There is no need to add to
the troubles each day brings."

Further Sayings

With 6:18 we come to the end of the more struc-
tured half of the Sermon on the Mount. In what follows,
the sayings of Jesus are woven together according to
major themes and key words, but we do not find the
tight numerical ordering of material. The sections might
even be considered meditations on the various petitions of the Our Father.

In 6:19–34, Jesus encourages his followers to live as
though the kingdom were already present. The detach-
ment and trust he calls for are not unusual attitudes for
one who believes that the world's order has come to an
end.

Verses 22–23 form a mysterious parable. Perhaps
they refer to our need to have our inner moral sense
enlightened by Christ's teaching in order to see the
passing nature of material possessions. This leads neatly
to verse 24 which is the heart of this whole section.
"Mammon" in verse 24 means "property." Matthew
does not deny that there are legitimate material concerns. He simply asks that believers put their priorities in
order.

Judging Others
(Also Luke 6.37–38, 41–42)

7 "Do not judge others, so that God will
not judge you—²because God will judge
you in the same way you judge others, and he
will apply to you the same rules you apply to
others. ³Why, then, do you look at the speck in
your brother's eye, and pay no attention to the

log in your own eye? ⁴How dare you say to your brother, 'Please, let me take that speck out of your eye,' when you have a log in your own eye? ⁵You impostor! Take the log out of your own eye first, and then you will be able to see and take the speck out of your brother's eye.

⁶"Do not give what is holy to dogs—they will only turn and attack you; do not throw your pearls in front of pigs—they will only trample them underfoot."

Ask, Seek, Knock
(Also Luke 11.9–13)

⁷"Ask, and you will receive; seek, and you will find; knock, and the door will be opened to you. ⁸For everyone who asks will receive, and he who seeks will find, and the door will be opened to him who knocks. ⁹Would any one of you fathers give his son a stone, when he asks you for bread? ¹⁰Or would you give him a snake, when he asks you for fish? ¹¹As bad as you are, you know how to give good things to your children. How much more, then, your Father in heaven will give good things to those who ask him!

¹²"Do for others what you want them to do for you: this is the meaning of the Law of Moses and the teaching of the prophets."

The Narrow Gate
(Also Luke 13.24)

¹³"Go in through the narrow gate, for the gate is wide and the road is easy that leads to hell, and there are many who travel it. ¹⁴The

gate is narrow and the way is hard that leads to life, and few people find it."

In chapter 7 the links between the various sayings and sections become even looser. We are told that, instead of judging, we should practice fraternal correction (7:3–5). The unclear parable in verse 6 may, however, place a limitation on fraternal correction: do not waste your time trying to give correction, or the Gospel itself, to people who are obviously ill-disposed and hostile.

Verses 7–11 form a call to constant and confident prayer. And yet these assurances run up against the hard fact that we do not always receive what we pray for. In the context of the previous teachings on prayer, however, Matthew is also calling us to trust in God's judgment rather than our own view of good.

Verse 12 is the famous "golden rule," well-known in the ancient world, pagan as well as Jewish. Although famous as a saying of Jesus, there is nothing uniquely Christian about it. Jews and pagans knew similar forms of the rule.

A Tree and Its Fruit
(Also Luke 6.43–44)

¹⁵"Watch out for false prophets; they come to you looking like sheep on the outside, but they are really like wild wolves on the inside. ¹⁶You will know them by the way they act. Thorn bushes do not bear grapes, and briars do not bear figs. ¹⁷A healthy tree bears good fruit, while a poor tree bears bad fruit. ¹⁸A healthy tree cannot bear bad fruit, and a poor tree cannot bear good fruit. ¹⁹Any tree that does not bear good fruit is cut down and thrown in

the fire. [20]So, then, you will know the false prophets by the way they act.''

I Never Knew You
(Also Luke 13.25—27)

[21]''Not every person who calls me 'Lord, Lord,' will enter into the Kingdom of heaven, but only those who do what my Father in heaven wants them to do. [22]When that Day comes, many will say to me, 'Lord, Lord! In your name we told God's message, by your name we drove out many demons and performed many miracles!' [23]Then I will say to them, 'I never knew you. Away from me, you evildoers!' ''

The Two House Builders
(Also Luke 6.47—49)

[24]''So then, everyone who hears these words of mine and obeys them will be like a wise man who built his house on the rock. [25]The rain poured down, the rivers flooded over, and the winds blew hard against that house. But it did not fall, because it had been built on the rock. [26]Everyone who hears these words of mine and does not obey them will be like a foolish man who built his house on the sand. [27]The rain poured down, the rivers flooded over, the winds flew hard against that house, and it fell. What a terrible fall that was!''

The Authority of Jesus

[28]Jesus finished saying these things, and the crowds were amazed at the way he taught.

²⁹He wasn't like their teachers of the Law; instead, he taught with authority.

False Prophets

The final section of the Sermon on the Mount (7:15–29) focuses on the final, either-or decision that must be made: the concrete doing of God's will or showy religiosity that adores one's own ego. Previously, Matthew spent a good amount of time attacking the Pharisees. Notice the enemies here are false disciples in the Church. The false prophets of verse 15 are Christian teachers who are powerful preachers with charismatic powers. They emphasize the attractive, flashy side of the Christian Gospel, while avoiding the hard demands of Christ.

In 7:21, the attack includes all charismatic types who work miracles and enjoy ecstacies, but who do not observe the day-to-day concrete moral demands Jesus makes on his disciples. For all their words, they do not *do* the works of love Jesus calls for. These Christians display the same sort of split in the religious person which we find in the Pharisees in 23:3–5.

The final parable of the Sermon (7:24–27) addresses not only Christian leaders, but also all Christians with a basic alternative: merely hearing, or both hearing and doing. The wise Christian is wise because he realizes he will face a stern judgment on the last day and so he "constructs" his Christian life accordingly.

The authority of the Israelite prophet came from his declaration: "The word of the Lord came to me, saying. . . ." The authority of the rabbi came from the chain of written and oral tradition passed down from generation to generation. Jesus' authority is not second hand.

He teaches on his own authority, depending on no other source for proof that his words are true.

Living the Ideal

Many people would read the Sermon on the Mount, praise its lofty ideals, and then go about the job of living in the real world, lacking in realizable ideals. Others would speak of the commands of the Sermon on the Mount as bringing to light the sad fact that we cannot live up to what God demands of us. They believe the purpose of the Sermon is to make us conscious of our sinfulness and to force us to our knees to beg God's mercy for our hopeless weakness. Still others say that Jesus intended these norms to be observed only for the short time which he thought remained before the end of the world. Such strenuous moral effort was possible for only a short period.

Matthew, however, takes the Sermon quite literally! He makes its ideal of doing rather than saying, and of acting on what is preached the proving ground for the true disciple. Too many of the "religious" Christians of his time fell into the same traps as the Pharisees and other Jewish leaders. Matthew assures us that, in the end, Jesus will judge us by the same standards he proclaimed in the Sermon on the Mount.

■ Reflection
In what ways do I live the ideals of the Sermon on the Mount in my everyday dealings with people?

■ Discussion

1. Does Matthew expect the true disciple to do what the Sermon on the Mount seems to demand?

2. Is it possible that the ideals in the Sermon on the Mount are realizable in the life of the Christian, but not in the world as a whole?

3. What do you think are Matthew's views on prayer, based on this section of the Gospel? Are they any different from those commonly held by Christians?

4. Based on your reading of the Sermon on the Mount, what do you think was Jesus' attitude toward material needs?

5. What picture of Christian community life is described in this section of Matthew's Gospel?

■ Prayer and Meditation

"The LORD says . . .
'Share your food with the hungry and open your hearts to the homeless poor. Give clothes to those who have nothing to wear, and do not refuse to help your own relatives.

'Then my favor will shine on you like the morning sun, and your wounds will be quickly healed. I will always be with you to save you; my presence will protect you on every side. When you pray, I will answer you. When you call to me, I will respond.' "

Isaiah 58:7–9

The Three Trios of Miracles —— Matthew 8:1—12:50

Just as Matthew drew together many different sayings of Jesus to create the rich compilation for the Sermon on the Mount, so now he draws together different miracle stories to form a portrait of Jesus the miracle worker.

Like the Sermon on the Mount, chapters 8 and 9 are well ordered. There are three groups of three miracles, each "trio" being set off from what follows by a "buffer section" of sayings. Most of the miracles are taken from Mark, although two are taken from the Q source. As we shall see, Matthew cuts down the Markan stories to their bare essentials. Matthew's miracle stories stress how a believer, who speaks the word of faith, encounters Jesus, who speaks the word of healing.

Jesus Heals a Man
(Also Mark 1.40—45; Luke 5.12—16)

8 Jesus came down from the hill, and large crowds followed him. ²Then a leper came to him, knelt down before him, and said, "Sir, if you want to, you can make me clean." ³Jesus reached out and touched him. "I do want to," he answered. "Be clean!" At once he was clean from his leprosy. ⁴Then Jesus said

to him: "Listen! Don't tell anyone, but go straight to the priest and let him examine you; then offer the sacrifice that Moses ordered, to prove to everyone that you are now clean."

Jesus Heals a Roman Officer's Servant
(Also Luke 7.1–10)

⁵When Jesus entered Capernaum, a Roman officer met him and begged for help: ⁶"'Sir, my servant is home sick in bed, unable to move, and suffering terribly." ⁷"I will go and make him well," Jesus said. ⁸"Oh no, sir," answered the officer. "I do not deserve to have you come into my house. Just give the order and my servant will get well. ⁹I, too, am a man with superior officers over me, and I have soldiers under me; so I order this one, 'Go!' and he goes; and I order that one, 'Come!' and he comes; and I order my slave, 'Do this!' and he does it." ¹⁰Jesus was surprised when he heard this, and said to the people who were following him: "I tell you, I have never seen such faith as this in anyone in Israel. ¹¹Remember this! Many will come from the east and the west and sit down at the table of the Kingdom of heaven with Abraham, Isaac, and Jacob. ¹²But those who should be in the Kingdom will be thrown out into the darkness outside, where they will cry and gnash their teeth." ¹³And Jesus said to the officer, "Go home, and what you believe will be done for you." And the officer's servant was healed that very hour.

¹⁴Jesus went to Peter's home, and there he saw Peter's mother-in-law sick in bed with a fever. ¹⁵He touched her hand; the fever left her, and she got up and began to wait on him.

¹⁶When evening came, people brought to Jesus many who had demons in them. Jesus drove out the evil spirits with a word and healed all who were sick. ¹⁷He did this to make come true what the prophet Isaiah had said, "He himself took our illnesses and carried away our diseases."

Miracles for Outcasts

The first trio of miracles extends from 8:1 to 8:17. Notice the three people affected by Jesus' miracles. Each one, a leper, a gentile, a woman, was excluded from fully participating in Jewish society or religious life. In the time of Christ, a "leper" would be anyone suffering from a skin disease. Such people were required to separate themselves from the community until they were pronounced cured by one of the priests. By touching the leper, Jesus became ritually defiled or unclean, and would not have been able to take part in public assemblies by law.

In Matthew, non-believers address Jesus as "teacher" or "rabbi"; believers address him as "Lord." The leper and the centurion both are thus placed in the category of believers. The centurion was in all likelihood a gentile, one of the Syrian troups stationed in Capernaum. He represented for Matthew those Christians not of Jewish birth or heritage.

Jesus' response in verses 11–12 does not seem to have belonged originally to this story. Luke has these words in a different context (Luke 13:28–29). Matthew includes both the unbelieving Jews and the Christians of his own Church who did not live up to the expectations of the kingdom.

The healing of Peter's mother-in-law is the only Matthean miracle story in which Jesus seizes the initiative instead of being petitioned by a believer. This is in keeping with the thrust of the quotation from Isaiah which follows in 8:17.

The Would-be Followers of Jesus
(Also Luke 9.57–62)

¹⁸Jesus noticed the crowd around him and gave orders to go to the other side of the lake. ¹⁹A teacher of the Law came to him. "Teacher," he said, "I am ready to go with you wherever you go." ²⁰Jesus answered him, "Foxes have holes, and birds have nests, but the Son of Man has no place to lie down and rest." ²¹Another man, who was a disciple, said, "Sir, first let me go and bury my father." ²²"Follow me," Jesus answered, "and let the dead bury their own dead."

The Cost of Discipleship

In Matthew 8:18–22, we have the first buffer section, which emphasizes the theme of the cost of discipleship. The first candidate for discipleship is a scribe who addresses Jesus as "teacher." Given Matthew's use of words, this tells us that the candidate is not a true believer. The candidate thinks he is showing a great generosity and openness to the demands of discipleship by his offer. Jesus indicates that to be his follower is not a matter of travel, but of suffering. Perhaps the would-be disciple is not equal to the task.

The title *Son of Man* occurs in Matthew twenty-nine times, with three basic references: 1) the earthly ministry; 2) the passion and resurrection; and 3) the last judgment. Here the first meaning is evident, perhaps looking to the second with its flavor of the cost of discipleship.

The second disciple addresses Jesus as "Lord," a sign that he is a true believer. Jesus encourages him to a deeper level of faith—to leave behind a "dead" world, including his family, as part of the price of discipleship.

Jesus Calms a Storm
(Also Mark 4.35–41; Luke 8.22–25)

[23]Jesus got into the boat, and his disciples went with him. [24]Suddenly a fierce storm hit the lake, so that the waves covered the boat. But Jesus was asleep. [25]The disciples went to him and woke him up. "Save us, Lord!" they said. "We are about to die!" [26]"Why are you so frightened?" Jesus answered. "How little faith you have!" Then he got up and gave a command to the winds and to the waves, and there was a great calm. [27]Everyone was amazed. "What kind of man is this?" they said. "Even the winds and the waves obey him!"

Jesus Heals Two Men with Demons
(Also Mark 5.1–20; Luke 8.26–39)

[28]Jesus came to the territory of the Gadarenes, on the other side of the lake, and was met by two men who came out of the burial caves. These men had demons in them and were very fierce, so dangerous that no one dared travel on that road. [29]At once they screamed, "What do you want with us, Son of God? Have you come to punish us before the right time?" [30]Not far away a large herd of pigs was feeding. [31]The demons begged Jesus, "If you are going to drive us out, send us into that herd of pigs." [32]"Go," Jesus told them; so they left and went off into the pigs. The whole herd rushed down the side of the cliff into the lake and were drowned.

³³The men who had been taking care of the pigs ran away and went to the town, where they told the whole story, and what had happened to the men with the demons. ³⁴So everybody from that town went out to meet Jesus; and when they saw him they begged him to leave their territory.

Jesus Quiets the Storm

The second trio of miracle stories stretches from 8:23—9:8. In the case of the stilling of the storm, it is very important to compare Matthew's version with Mark 4:35—41. Almost every change Matthew makes stresses one of his themes: the majesty of Jesus, the cost of discipleship, the need for greater faith. In Matthew, Jesus seizes the initiative by getting into the boat. There is a clear message in this story for the members of Matthew's Church. Jesus is in charge from the beginning. The "fierce storm" is better translated as "earthquake," a sign of the coming of the kingdom. Matthew describes earthquakes at both the crucifixion and the resurrection. As long as Jesus is with them, they need not fear the turmoil they experience as members of a fledgling Church in the midst of opposition. If they abandon hope in him, the boat (Church) will be lost.

In the story of the demoniacs, the number of verses Mark gives over to the possessed is severely cut by Matthew. They drop out of the narrative as soon as they are exorcised. The devils want to bargain for some "time" and (for *them*) "decent living conditions." Accordingly, they ask permission to enter the swine (unclean "pagan" animals). Jesus' apparent permission actually stresses his supreme control of the situation and his victory over evil. The focus of the story is clearly the power of Jesus over the evil spirits who recognize him as the Son of God.

■ Reflection

How do events in today's Church show our trust (or lack of it) in Jesus' ability to sustain and guide our community?

Jesus Heals a Paralyzed Man
(Also Mark 2.1–12; Luke 5.17–26)

9 Jesus got into the boat, went back across the lake, and came to his own town. ²Some people brought him a paralyzed man, lying on a bed. Jesus saw how much faith they had, and said to the paralyzed man, "Courage, my son! Your sins are forgiven." ³Then some teachers of the Law said to themselves, "This man is talking against God!" ⁴Jesus knew what they were thinking and said: "Why are you thinking such evil things? ⁵Is it easier to say, 'Your sins are forgiven,' or to say 'Get up and walk'? ⁶I will prove to you, then that the Son of Man has authority on earth to forgive sins." So he said to the paralyzed man, "Get up, pick up your bed, and go home!" ⁷The man got up and went home. ⁸When the people saw it, they were afraid, and praised God for giving such authority as this to men.

Forgiveness of Sins

In the story of the paralytic (9:1–8), Jesus is dealing with two audiences at the same time. He sees the evil in the hearts of the scribes as clearly as he sees evil in the paralytic. The charge of blasphemy against Jesus is of utmost importance for the outcome of Matthew's Gospel. It is this charge that ultimately results in his death. All the evidence in Matthew points to the fact that the charge is false. Jesus counters his enemies' charge in true rabbinic fashion by asking a question about the comparative difficulty of two types of "sayings." As Jesus heals the paralytic, he describes himself as "the Son of Man," here in the sense of his earthly ministry. Jesus' authority is again emphasized. He is the one who can forgive sins.

Jesus Calls Matthew
(Also Mark 2.13–17; Luke 5.27–32)

⁹Jesus left that place, and as he walked along he saw a tax collector, named Matthew, sitting in his office. He said to him, "Follow me." And Matthew got up and followed him.

¹⁰While Jesus was having dinner at his house, many tax collectors and outcasts came and joined him and his disciples at the table. ¹¹Some Pharisees saw this and said to his disciples, "Why does your teacher eat with tax collectors and outcasts?" ¹²Jesus heard them and answered: "People who are well do not need a doctor, but only those who are sick. ¹³Go and find out what this scripture means, 'I do not want animal sacrifices, but kindness.' For I have not come to call the respectable people, but the outcasts."

The Question About Fasting
(Also Mark 2.18–22; Luke 5.33–39)

¹⁴Then the followers of John the Baptist came to Jesus, asking, "Why is it that we and the Pharisees fast often, but your disciples don't fast at all?" ¹⁵Jesus answered: "Do you expect the guests at a wedding party to be sad as long as the bridegroom is with them? Of course not! But the time will come when the bridegroom will be taken away from them, and then they will go without food.

While the first buffer section spoke of the cost of discipleship, the second buffer section (9:9–17) speaks of the joy of discipleship. The events of this buffer section flow smoothly from the last miracle account, referring as it does to sickness and sinfulness. Tax collectors were considered to be sinners because of their dealings with the Romans and the suspicion that they collected more than was required.

Since in Matthew the disciples are identified with the Twelve, he identifies the tax collector as the apostle Matthew (Mark and Luke give his name as Levi). There was no historical person with the double name Levi-Matthew, so we can conclude that the author of Matthew's Gospel is not writing about himself. If he were, he would not be depending on Mark for the story of his calling.

Jesus' answer to the Pharisees' objection to the reputation of his dinner guests relates again to the theme of healing over the observance of the law. The real "sinners" here are on the side of the law. The quote from Hosea 6:6 points out their misunderstanding of God's will.

The answer of Jesus to the question about fasting should be treated in two parts. "Do you expect the guests at a wedding party to be sad as long as the bridegroom is with them?" probably comes from the historical Jesus, who rejected traditional Jewish pieties like fasting. The second half of verse 15 is probably an addition of the early Church, justifying the resumption of the practice of fasting in the post-resurrection period.

---

[16]"No one patches up an old coat with a piece of new cloth; for such a patch tears off from the coat, making an even bigger hole. [17]Nor does anyone pour new wine into used

wineskins. If he does, the skins will burst, and then the wine pours out and the skins will be ruined. Instead, new wine is poured into fresh wineskins, and both will keep in good condition."

The Official's Daughter and the Woman Who Touched Jesus' Cloak
(Also Mark 5.21–43; Luke 8.40–56)

[18]While Jesus was saying this to them, a Jewish official came to him, knelt down before him, and said, "My daughter has just died; but come and place your hand on her and she will live." [19]So Jesus got up and followed him, and his disciples went with him.

[20]A certain woman, who had had severe bleeding for twelve years, came up behind Jesus and touched the edge of his cloak. [21]She said to herself, "If only I touch his cloak I will get well." [22]Jesus turned around and saw her, and said, "Courage, my daughter! Your faith has made you well." At that very moment the woman became well.

[23]So Jesus went into the official's house. When he saw the musicians for the funeral, and the people all stirred up, [24]he said, "Get out, everybody! The little girl is not dead—she is just sleeping!" They all started making fun of him. [25]As soon as the people had been put out, Jesus went into the girl's room and took hold of her hand, and she got up. [26]The news about this spread all over that part of the country.

[27]Jesus left that place, and as he walked along two blind men started following him. "Have mercy on us, Son of David!" they

The basic instructions for the limited mission to Israel are given in 10:5–16. The narrow restrictions of the mission might have been used by conservative Jewish Christians to argue against a gentile mission. Matthew is able to preserve this tradition by referring it, and restricting it, to the time of Jesus' earthly ministry. For Matthew, the death-resurrection will open up a new period, when the risen Jesus commands the same group of disciples to undertake a world-wide mission. Matthew's radicalism is seen in his prohibition of any extra supplies or aids. The missionaries can waive supplies, because those who have the right heart to believe their message will also receive the messenger hospitably. The dynamic word of the messenger will confer the greater gift of peace. That same word, if rejected, will leave the unbelieving town to a fearful fate on the last day. Refusal to believe in Jesus will make the Jews more liable to judgment than even the unclean pagans.

---

[17] "Watch out, for there will be men who will arrest you and take you to court, and they will whip you in their synagogues. [18]You will be brought to trial before rulers and kings for my sake, to tell the Good News to them and to the Gentiles. [19]When they bring you to trial, do not worry about what you are going to say or how you will say it; when the time comes, you will be given what you will say. [20]For the words you speak will not be yours; they will come from the Spirit of your Father speaking in you.

[21]"Men will hand over their own brothers to be put to death, and fathers will do the same to their children; children will turn against their parents and have them put to death. [22]Everyone will hate you, because of me. But the person who holds out to the end will be saved.

²³And when they persecute you in one town, run away to another one. I tell you, you will not finish your work in all the towns of Israel before the Son of Man comes.

²⁴"No pupil is greater than his teacher; no slave is greater than his master. ²⁵So a pupil should be satisfied to become like his teacher, and a slave like his master. If the head of the family is called Beelzebul, the members of the family will be called by even worse names!"

The Risk of Discipleship

The mission means risk and danger—not only for the audience, but also for the missionaries, and indeed for all disciples. In 10:17–25, future persecution is predicted not only for missionaries but also for all believers. The horizons of the discourse expand to take in the lot of all Christians in the period after the resurrection. At this point Matthew borrows from Mark's eschatological discourse (Mark 13) to give the future, world-wide mission a fittingly cosmic and apocalyptic tone. The disciples' fate closely follows that of Jesus in his passion. Like Jesus, they will not be forsaken by their Father. Since they are children of the Father, the Father's Spirit will guide them, strengthening them to endure "to the end" (the "eschaton"), the coming of the Son of Man to judge. Even though the disciples may be forced to flee for their lives from city to city, they are not to lose heart. The Son of Man is coming soon to grant them rescue and salvation.

Whom to Fear
(Also Luke 12.2–7)

²⁶"Do not be afraid of men, then. Whatever is covered up will be uncovered, and every secret will be made known. ²⁷What I am telling

you in the dark you must repeat in broad daylight, and what you have heard in private you must tell from the housetops. [28]Do not be afraid of those who kill the body but cannot kill the soul; rather be afraid of God, who can destroy both body and soul in hell. [29]You can buy two sparrows for a penny; yet not a single one of them falls to the ground without your Father's consent. [30]As for you, even the hairs of your head have all been counted. [31]So do not be afraid: you are worth much more than sparrows!''

[32]''Whoever declares publicly that he belongs to me, I will do the same for him before my Father in heaven. [33]But whoever denies publicly that he belongs to me, then I will deny him before my Father in heaven.''

Not Peace, but a Sword
(Also Luke 12.51–53; 14.26–27)

[34]''Do not think that I have come to bring peace to the world; no, I did not come to bring peace, but a sword. [35]I came to set sons against their fathers, daughters against their mothers, daughters-in-law against their mothers-in-law; [36] a man's worst enemies will be the members of his own family.

[37]''Whoever loves his father or mother more than me is not worthy of me; whoever loves his son or daughter more than me is not worthy of me. [38]Whoever does not take up his cross and follow in my steps is not worthy of me. [39]Whoever tries to gain his own life will lose it; whoever loses his life for my sake will gain it.''

[40]''Whoever welcomes you, welcomes me; and whoever welcomes me, welcomes the one who sent me. [41]Whoever welcomes God's mes-

senger because he is God's messenger will share in his reward; and whoever welcomes a truly good man, because he is that, will share in his reward. ⁴²And remember this! Whoever gives even a drink of cold water to one of the least of these my followers, because he is my follower, will certainly receive his reward.''

Therefore, the disciples must be fearless as they face persecution (10:26–33). Three times Jesus repeats: Fear not! The violence of their persecutors cannot suppress the message or rob the disciples of eternal life. Fear betrays a lack of faith in their provident Father, who knows their slightest need. If the disciples bear witness to Jesus before earthly courts, Jesus the Son of Man will bear witness to them in final, heavenly court. Earthly fear will bring final rejection. The cost of discipleship is high: hatred and even martyrdom at the hands of one's family (10:34–39). Yet the rewards of discipleship are greater (10:40–11:1). Listening to the preachers of the Christian community, or even simply helping one of the ordinary members of the community, will be rewarded by the all-provident Father. Matthew's usual formula concludes the second discourse (11:1).

The Messengers from John the Baptist
(Also Luke 7.18–35)

11 When Jesus finished giving these instructions to his twelve disciples, he left that place and went on to teach and preach in the towns near there.

²When John the Baptist heard in prison about Christ's works, he sent some of his disciples to him. ³"Tell us,'' they asked Jesus, ''are you the one John said was going to come, or should we expect someone else?'' ⁴Jesus an-

swered: "Go back and tell John what you are hearing and seeing: [5]the blind can see, the lame can walk, the lepers are made clean, the deaf hear, the dead are raised to life, and the Good News is preached to the poor. [6]How happy is he who has no doubts about me!"

[7]While John's disciples were going back, Jesus spoke about John to the crowds. "When you went out to John in the desert, what did you expect to see? A blade of grass bending in the wind? [8]What did you go out to see? A man dressed up in fancy clothes? People who dress like that live in palaces! [9]Tell me, what did you expect to see? A prophet? Yes, I tell you—you saw much more than a prophet. [10]For John is the one of whom the scripture says: 'Here is my messenger, says God; I will send him ahead of you to open the way for you.' [11]Remember this! John the Baptist is greater than any man who has ever lived. But he who is least in the Kingdom of heaven is greater than he. [12]From the time John preached his message until this very day the Kingdom of heaven has suffered violent attacks, and violent men try to seize it. [13]All the prophets and the Law of Moses, until the time of John, spoke about the Kingdom; [14]and if you are willing to believe their message, John is Elijah, whose coming was predicted. Listen, then, if you have ears!

[16]"Now, to what can I compare the people of this day? They are like children sitting in the marketplace. One group shouts to the other, [17]'We played wedding music for you, but you would not dance! We sang funeral songs, but you would not cry!' [18]John came, and he fasted and drank no wine, and everyone said, 'He is a madman!' [19]The Son of Man came, and he ate and drank, and everyone said, 'Look at this man! He is a glutton and wine-drinker, and is a

friend of tax collectors and outcasts!' God's wisdom, however, is shown to be true by its results."

The Unbelieving Towns
(Also Luke 10.13—15)

[20]Then Jesus began to reproach the towns where he had performed most of his miracles, because the people had not turned from their sins. [21]"How terrible it will be for you, Chorazin! How terrible for you, too, Bethsaida! For if the miracles which were performed in you had been performed in Tyre and Sidon, long ago, the people there would have put on sackcloth, and sprinkled ashes on themselves to show they had turned from their sins! [22]Remember, then, that on the Judgment Day God will show more mercy to the people of Tyre and Sidon than to you! [23]And as for you, Capernaum! You wanted to lift yourself up to heaven? You will be thrown down to hell! For if the miracles which were performed in you had been performed in Sodom, it would still be in existence today! [24]Remember, then, that on the Judgment Day God will show more mercy to Sodom than to you!"

Come to Me and Rest
(Also Luke 10.21—22)

[25]At that time Jesus said: "O Father, Lord of heaven and earth! I thank you because you have shown to the unlearned what you have hidden from the wise and learned. [26]Yes, Father, this was done by your own choice and pleasure.

²⁷"My Father has given me all things. No one knows the Son except the Father, and no one knows the Father except the Son, and those to whom the Son wants to reveal him.

²⁸"Come to me, all of you who are tired from carrying your heavy loads, and I will give you rest. ²⁹Take my yoke and put it on you, and learn from me, for I am gentle and humble in spirit; and you will find rest. ³⁰The yoke I will give you is easy, and the load I will put on you is light."

Belief in Jesus

Chapters 11 and 12 form the narrative part of book three of the ministry (11:2—12:53). In this book, the tension and conflict between Jesus and his own people, Israel, heighten almost to the breaking point. The tone of struggle against disbelief is set at the opening, by the bewildered question of the Baptist. The Jesus who teaches and heals did not seem to fulfill John's prophecy of a fiery judge. John asks whether Jesus really is the coming one, the Messiah. Jesus answers by pointing to the fact that Jesus' merciful ministry perfectly fulfills the Old Testament prophecies. Jesus hints to the Baptist that the greatest messianic blessing of all is not to let the disconcerting merciful style of this Messiah keep one from faith.

In 11:7—19, Jesus, having answered the question of who he is, asks the crowds who the Baptist is. By rhetorical questions (questions with built-in answers), Jesus excludes the possibilities of his being either a vacillating time-server or a powerful politician. John was a prophet—and yet more. He was a prophet who lived to see all prophecy fulfilled in Jesus. Indeed, John is Elijah. But neither Elijah nor the Messiah he heralds has been accepted by the finicky, childish Israelites, who always find some reason for ignoring both the ascetic and the bearer of glad tidings. In 11:20–24, Jesus responds sharply to this rejection by proclaiming judgment on the Galilean cities which have seen his miracles and not believed. Having been granted special blessings, they will receive special punishment, worse than what will befall the wicked cities of the Old Testament. By way of contrast, Jesus praises and thanks his Father for granting revelation and the grace of faith to Jesus' humble disciples (11:25–30). The content of this revelation is the mutual, unique relationship between the Father and Son. Jesus, the unique Son, grants a share in his relationship with the Father to all who accept him in faith. Speaking like a personified Wisdom in the Old Testament, Jesus invites all the "little ones" of this world to accept the "rest" he offers, the law he teaches, which is none other than Jesus himself.

The Question About the Sabbath
(Also Mark 2.23–28; Luke 6.1–5)

12 Not long afterward Jesus was walking through the wheat fields on a Sabbath day. His disciples were hungry, so they began to pick heads of wheat and eat the grain. ²When the Pharisees saw this, they said to Jesus, "Look, it is against our Law for your disciples to do this on the Sabbath!" ³Jesus answered: "Have you never read what David did that time when he and his men were hungry? ⁴He went into the house of God, and he and his men ate the bread offered to God, even though it was against the Law for them to eat that bread—only the priests were allowed to eat it. ⁵Or have you not read in the Law of Moses that every Sabbath the priests in the Temple actually break the Sabbath law, yet they are not guilty? ⁶There is something here, I tell you, greater than the Temple. ⁷If you really knew what this scripture means, 'I do not want animal sacrifices, but kindness,' you would not condemn people who are guilty. ⁸For the Son of Man is Lord of the Sabbath.''

⁹Jesus left that place and went to one of their synagogues. ¹⁰A man was there who had a crippled hand. There were some men present who wanted to accuse Jesus of wrongdoing; so they asked him, ''Is it against our Law to cure on the Sabbath?'' ¹¹Jesus answered: ''What if one of you has a sheep and it falls into a deep hole on the Sabbath? Will you not take hold of it and lift it out? ¹²And a man is worth much more than a sheep! So, then, our Law does allow us to help someone on the Sabbath.'' ¹³Then he said to the man, ''Stretch out your hand.'' He stretched it out, and it became well again, just like the other one. ¹⁴The Pharisees left and made plans against Jesus to kill him.

The Sabbath

The tone of conflict grows stronger in chapter 12. Jesus' teaching about Sabbath-rest opens the first of two disputes on the Sabbath. Jesus defends the plucking of grain by his disciples (12:1–8) by appealing to the actions of David and of the Temple priests. More importantly, Jesus appeals to the great teaching of the prophets: God wants mercy more than ritual observance (see Hosea 6:6). Jesus, the merciful Son of Man, is the true interpreter of God's will as regards the Sabbath and the whole law.

The second dispute on a Sabbath (12:9–14) combines a debate over teaching with a miracle. Both Jesus' argumentation over what is lawful on the Sabbath (obviously, mercy towards one in need) and his acting out of his teaching by healing cause the Pharisees to plot his death.

God's Chosen Servant

[15]When Jesus heard about it, he went away from that place; and many people followed him. He healed all the sick, [16]and gave them orders not to tell others about him, [17]to make come true what the prophet Isaiah had said:

> [18]"Here is my servant, says God, whom I have chosen,
>> The one I love, with whom I am well pleased.
>> I will put my Spirit on him,
>> And he will announce my judgment to all people.
> [19]But he will not argue or shout,
>> Nor will he make loud speeches in the streets;
> [20]He will not break off a bent reed,
>> Nor will he put out a flickering lamp.
>> He will persist until he causes justice to triumph;
> [21]And all people will put their hope in him."

Jesus and Beelzebul
(Also Mark 3.20—30; Luke 11.14—23)

[22]Then some people brought to Jesus a man who was blind and could not talk because he had a demon. Jesus healed the man, so that he was able to talk and see. [23]The crowds were all amazed. "Could he be the Son of David?" they asked. [24]When the Pharisees heard this they replied, "He drives out demons only because their ruler Beelzebul gives him power to do so."

[25]Jesus knew what they were thinking and said to them: "Any country that divides itself into groups that fight each other will not last very long. And any town or family that divides itself into groups that fight each other will fall apart. [26]So if one group is fighting another in Satan's kingdom, this means that it is already divided into groups and will soon fall apart! [27]You say that I drive out demons because Beelzebul gives me the power to do so. Well, then, who gives your followers the power to drive them out? Your own followers prove that you are completely wrong! [28]No, it is God's Spirit who gives me the power to drive out demons, which proves that the Kingdom of God has already come upon you.

[29]"No one can break into a strong man's house and take away his belongings unless he ties up the strong man first; then he can plunder his house.

[30]"Anyone who is not for me is really against me; anyone who does not help me gather is really scattering. [31]For this reason I tell you: men can be forgiven any sin and any evil thing they say; but whoever says evil things against the Holy Spirit will not be forgiven. [32]Anyone who says something against the Son of Man will be forgiven; but whoever says something against the Holy Spirit will not be forgiven—now or ever."

A Tree and Its Fruit
(Also Luke 6.43—45)

[33]"To have good fruit you must have a healthy tree; if you have a poor tree you will have bad fruit. For a tree is known by the kind of fruit it bears. [34]You snakes—how can you

say good things when you are evil? For the mouth speaks what the heart is full of. [35]A good man brings good things out of his treasure of good things; a bad man brings bad things out of his treasure of bad things.

[36]"And I tell you this: on the Judgment Day everyone will have to give account of every useless word he has ever spoken. [37]For your words will be used to judge you, either to declare you innocent or to declare you guilty."

Jesus' response to this opposition (12:15–21) is to withdraw temporarily from the heat of battle. This withdrawal displays not weakness or fear but Jesus' status as a peaceable servant of the Lord, prophesied by Isaiah 42:1–4. Even Israel's opposition is not an unmitigated tragedy; the mercy of the servant will be directed instead to the gentiles. The intensity of the Pharisees' opposition is seen in the fact that they refer even Jesus' merciful healing of a blind and mute demoniac to the power of demons (12:22–37). Jesus shows how absurd it would be for Satan to destroy his own empire. Jesus' exorcisms foretell and make present even now his definitive victory over evil. Jesus then attacks the Pharisees, warning them that, if they willfully close their eyes to the clear working of God's Spirit, they will forfeit all hope of salvation. When some Pharisees counter with a request for some spectacular, legitimizing miracle, Jesus refuses to give it (12:38–45). The Pharisees have received a greater revelation than any of the well-disposed people of the Old Testament, and yet in their malice they still demand more. The only sign Jesus will give is the sign of his own death and resurrection. Yet even that sign will be rejected by most of Israel, and so its final state will be worse than its state before Jesus' ministry.

The Demand for a Miracle
(Also Mark 8.11—12; Luke 11.29—32)

[38]Then some teachers of the Law and some Pharisees spoke up. "Teacher," they said, "we want to see you perform a miracle." [39]"How evil and godless are the people of this day!" Jesus exclaimed. "You ask me for a miracle? No! The only miracle you will be given is the miracle of the prophet Jonah. [40]In the same way that Jonah spent three days and nights in the belly of the big fish, so will the Son of Man spend three days and nights in the depths of the earth. [41]On the Judgment Day the people of Nineveh will stand up and accuse you, because they turned from their sins when they heard Jonah preach; and there is something here, I tell you, greater than Jonah! [42]On the Judgment Day the Queen from the South will stand up and accuse you, because she traveled halfway around the world to listen to Solomon's wise teaching; and there is something here, I tell you, greater than Solomon!"

The Return of the Evil Spirit
(Also Luke 11.24—26)

[43]"When an evil spirit goes out of a man, it travels over dry country looking for a place to rest. If it can't find one, [44]it says to itself, 'I will go back to my house which I left.' So it goes back and finds it empty, clean, and all fixed up. [45]Then it goes out and brings along seven other spirits even worse than itself, and they come and live there. So that man is in worse shape, when it is all over, than he was at the beginning. This is the way it will happen to the evil people of this day."

Jesus' Mother and Brothers
(Also Mark 3.31–35; Luke 8.19–21)

⁴⁶Jesus was still talking to the people when his mother and brothers arrived. They stood outside, asking to speak with him. ⁴⁷So one of the people there said to him, "Look, your mother and brothers are standing outside, and they want to speak with you." ⁴⁸Jesus answered, "Who is my mother? Who are my brothers?" ⁴⁹Then he pointed to his disciples and said: "Look! Here are my mother and my brothers! ⁵⁰For the person who does what my Father in heaven wants him to do is my brother, my sister, my mother."

The theme of opposition and conflict concludes with Jesus' rejection of any claim of blood ties (12:46–50). Jesus' true family is made up of believers. His earthly mother and brothers are left "outside" because the family-ties of this world carry no weight in the kingdom.

■ Reflection
How has it happened that some "religious" elements have been characterized as being opposed to the Gospel message in today's society?

■ Discussion
1. What overall purpose do the miracle stories serve in Matthew's Gospel? In what ways do they enhance our understanding of Jesus' message?
2. Considering that miracle stories in the Gospels are carefully chosen by the evangelists to emphasize theological ideas, is it important to know whether they have any actual historical foundation?

3. What are the joys and the dangers of becoming a true disciple of Jesus?

4. What factors, do you think, are at the root of the Pharisees' opposition to Jesus?

5. Why is it that some (the disciples) were quick to understand and accept Jesus' message, and others continued to be hostile to the same message?

■ Prayer and Meditation

"For this reason I remind you to keep alive the gift that God gave you when I laid my hands on you. For the Spirit that God has given us does not make us timid; instead, his Spirit fills us with power, love, and self-control. Do not be ashamed, then, of witnessing for our Lord."

2 Timothy 1:6–8

The Parables Split Israel — Matthew 13:1—18:35

The whole of book three has emphasized the growing tension, the widening gap, between Jesus and his disciples on the one hand and the Jewish leaders on the other. We are not too surprised, therefore, that the discourse of book three hammers home this theme of increasing division. What is perhaps more surprising for us is that Matthew has chosen to use a discourse made up of parables as the expression of heightened tension and imminent break. For many of us, parables conjure up the idea of simple, homey stories which Jesus used to make his message clear to ordinary people. That is *not* Matthew's understanding of parables. For him, parables are mysterious stories or riddles which cannot be understood without God's grace and the explanation of Jesus.

Parables

This interpretation of the parables is not without foundation in the historical Jesus himself. Parables were an honored tradition in the wisdom teaching of Israel. A parable could be any sort of statement or a wise insight, ranging from a short maxim to a short story. Jesus used parables which were often mysterious and riddle-like. Instead of being immediately clear in their meaning, they were mind-teasers, calling for thought and decision on the part of the listeners. In their tendency to turn ordinary values and expectations upside down, the parables attacked the accepted way of thinking and acting, and challenged their audience to dare to open themselves up to the new world of God's values and actions.

Both Mark and Matthew could seize upon the mysterious, veiled meaning of the parables and use it for their own purposes—Mark for his theory of the "messianic secret," Matthew for his view of the growing split between Jesus and Israel. But in reinterpreting Jesus' parables, the evangelists were doing nothing new. The early Church before them had already begun the process of reinterpreting and allegorizing the parables of Jesus. Therefore, as we read these parables, we must be aware of three different possible levels of meaning: the meaning the historical Jesus intended, the reinterpretation given by the early Church, and the further reinterpretation given by the evangelists.

The Parable of the Sower
(Also Mark 4.1–9; Luke 8.4–8)

13 That same day Jesus left the house and went to the lakeside, where he sat down to teach. ²The crowd that gathered around him was so large that he got into a boat and sat in it, while the crowd stood on the shore. ³He used parables to tell them many things.

"There was a man who went out to sow. ⁴As he scattered the seed in the field, some of it fell along the path, and the birds came and ate it up. ⁵Some of it fell on rocky ground, where there was little soil. The seeds soon sprouted, because the soil wasn't deep. ⁶When the sun came up it burned the young plants, and because the roots had not grown deep enough the plants soon dried up. [7]Some of the seed fell among thorns, which grew up and choked the plants. [8]But some seeds fell in good soil, and bore grain: some had one hundred grains, others sixty, and others thirty." [9]And Jesus said, "Listen, then, if you have ears!"

The Purpose of the Parables
(Also Mark 4.10–12; Luke 8.9–10)

[10]Then the disciples came to Jesus and asked him, "Why do you use parables when you talk to them?" [11]"The knowledge of the secrets of the Kingdom of heaven has been given to you," Jesus answered, "but not to them. [12]For the man who has something will be given more, so that he will have more than enough; but the man who has nothing will have taken away from him even the little he has. [13]This is the reason that I use parables to talk to them: it is because they look, but do not see, and they listen, but do not hear or understand. [14]So the prophecy of Isaiah comes true in their case:

'You will listen and listen, but not understand;
You will look and look, but not see.
[15]Because this people's mind is dull;
They have stopped up their ears,
And they have closed their eyes.
Otherwise, their eyes might see,
Their ears might hear,
Their minds might understand
And they might turn to me, says God,
And I would heal them.'

[16]As for you, how fortunate you are! Your eyes see and your ears hear. [17]Remember this! Many prophets and many of God's people

wanted very much to see what you see, but they could not, and to hear what you hear, but they did not."

[18]"Listen, then, and learn what the parable of the sower means. [19]Those who hear the message about the Kingdom but do not understand it are like the seed that fell along the path. The Evil One comes and snatches away what was sown in them. [20]The seed that fell on rocky ground stands for those who receive the message gladly as soon as they hear it. [21]But it does not sink deep in them, and they don't last long. So when trouble or persecution comes because of the message, they give up at once. [22]The seed that fell among thorns stands for those who hear the message, but the worries about this life and the love for riches choke the message, and they don't bear fruit. [23]And the seed sown in the good soil stands for those who hear the message and understand it: they bear fruit, some as much as one hundred, others sixty, and others thirty."

The Parable of the Weeds

[24]Jesus told them another parable: "The Kingdom of heaven is like a man who sowed good seed in his field. [25]One night, when everyone was asleep, an enemy came and sowed weeds among the wheat, and went away. [26]When the plants grew and the heads of grain began to form, then the weeds showed up. [27]The man's servants came to him and said, 'Sir, it was good seed you sowed in your field; where did the weeds come from?' [28]'It was some enemy who did this,' he answered. 'Do you want us to go and pull up the weeds?' they asked him. [29]'No,' he answered, 'because as you gather the

weeds you might pull up some of the wheat along with them. ³⁰Let the wheat and the weeds both grow together until harvest, and then I will tell the harvest workers: Pull up the weeds first and tie them in bundles to throw in the fire; then gather in the wheat and put it in my barn.' "

The Parable of the Mustard Seed
(Also Mark 4.30–32; Luke 13.18–19)

³¹Jesus told them another parable: "The Kingdom of heaven is like a mustard seed, the smallest of all seeds; ³²a man takes it and sows it in his field, and when it grows up it is the biggest of all plants. It becomes a tree, so that the birds come and make their nests in its branches."

³³Jesus told them another parable: "The Kingdom of heaven is like yeast. A woman takes it and mixes it with a bushel of flour, until the whole batch of dough rises."

³⁴Jesus used parables to tell all these things to the crowds; he would not say a thing to them without using a parable. ³⁵He did this to make come true what the prophet had said:
"I will use parables when I speak to them,
I will tell them things unknown since the creation of the world."

We can see Matthew's orderly hand in the fact that his parable chapter is made up of seven parables, divided into two major sections. The great dividing line is 13:36, when Jesus leaves the crowds, and henceforth speaks only to his disciples. In the first major section (13:1–35) Matthew places the parable of the sower;

Jesus' reason for speaking in parables; the explanation of the parable of the sower; the parable of the wheat and the weeds; the parables of the mustard seed and the leaven; joined to a concluding remark about the use of parables. In the second major section, after Jesus leaves the crowds, Matthew gives us the explanation of the parable of the wheat and the weeds, the two parables of the treasure and the pearl, and the final parable of the fishnet.

In 13:1, Matthew notes that the parable discourse is given "that same day"—presumably on the same day as the events in chapter 12. The house Jesus leaves is the house his relatives were not allowed to enter. Jesus "sits" by the seashore. This action, as in the Sermon on the Mount, prepares us for Jesus' words as a teacher.

The Sower

While we have heard a few short parables from Jesus before this (for example, 5:13–16), the parable of the sower is the first parable of notable length in Matthew's Gospel. In ancient Palestine, a great amount of seed was prodigally cast about in the field, and a great deal seemed to be wasted. Yet the seed that did take root produced an abundant harvest—indeed, Jesus exaggerates the abundance at the end of the parable. Jesus expresses in this parable the confidence that he had in the success of his preaching. Jesus is the sower. He spreads his message freely. Despite opposition, it bears fruit in abundance.

The next paragraph, verses 10 to 17, interrupts the flow of the parables, and poses a difficulty. The disciples ask why Jesus speaks to them—the crowds—in parables. The crowds represent Israel which has refused to understand Jesus' message. God has established a division between the disciples and the crowd, because he has given understanding to the disciples. The disciples are the true believers. Matthew emphasizes the point by having Jesus speak a formula quotation (Isaiah 6:9–10). Jesus contrasts the disciples with Israel which Isaiah describes. The disciples are part of the kingdom which the prophets of Israel were not privileged to see.

The explanation of the parable of the sower is given in 13:18–23. The explanation is actually an allegorical interpretation of the parable supplied by the early Church. Notice how the allegory is not even consistent in itself. The seed, which originally meant the word of the kingdom, now represents different kinds of Christians in the early Church. Many hear the word and accept the Church, but cannot live up the the task of discipleship.

The Wheat and the Weeds

Having finished with the explanation of one parable, Matthew introduces another parable which will later receive a lengthy explanation. The parable of the wheat and the weeds is a parable which occurs only in Matthew and reflects typically Matthean concerns. It is interesting to see this parable as a "fleshing out" of the parable of the sower. The sower has now become a householder, and the forces of opposing the growth of the seed are partly personified (the enemy) and partly unified as one type of poisonous weed (darnel). The Church will always contain both faithful and unfaithful members. They are so intermingled at the root that Matthew recommends through the householder that they need not be separated until the day of judgment.

■ Reflection
How would you apply the parables of the sower and the wheat and the weeds to today's Church?

Jesus Explains the Parable of the Weeds

[36]Then Jesus left the crowd and went indoors. His disciples came to him and said, "Tell us what the parable of the weeds in the field means." [37]Jesus answered: "The man who sowed the good seed is the Son of Man; [38]the field is the world; the good seed is the people who belong to the Kingdom; the weeds are the people who belong to the Evil One; [39]and the enemy who sowed the weeds is the Devil himself. The harvest is the end of the age, and the harvest workers are angels. [40]Just as the weeds are gathered up and burned in the fire, so it will be at the end of the age: [41]the Son of Man will send out his angels and they will gather up out of his Kingdom all who cause people to sin, and all other evildoers, [42]and throw them into the fiery furnace, where they will cry and gnash their teeth. [43]Then God's people will shine like the sun in their Father's Kingdom. Listen, then, if you have ears!"

[44]"The Kingdom of heaven is like a treasure hidden in a field. A man happens to find it, so he covers it up again. He is so happy that he goes and sells everything he has, and then goes back and buys the field."

The Parable of the Pearl

[45]"Also, the Kingdom of heaven is like a buyer looking for fine pearls. [46]When he finds one that is unusually fine, he goes and sells everything he has, and buys the pearl."

[47]"Also, the Kingdom of heaven is like a net thrown out in the lake, which catches all kinds

of fish. ⁴⁸When it is full, the fishermen pull it to shore and sit down to divide the fish: the good ones go into their buckets, the worthless ones are thrown away. ⁴⁹It will be like this at the end of the age: the angels will go out and gather up the evil people from among the good, ⁵⁰and throw them into the fiery furnace. There they will cry and gnash their teeth."

New Truths and Old

⁵¹"Do you understand these things?" Jesus asked them. "Yes," they answered. ⁵²So he replied, "This means, then, that every teacher of the Law who becomes a disciple in the Kingdom of heaven is like a homeowner who takes new and old things out of his storage room."

In 13:36, Jesus leaves the crowds and goes into his house. It is now midway through the Gospel, and this action is symbolic of Jesus separating himself from Israel to devote himself to teaching the disciples, who are receptive to the message of the kingdom.

The Treasure, the Pearl, the Fishnet

The twin parables of the treasure and the pearl, following the explanation of the parable of the wheat and the weeds, remind us, as far as form is concerned, of the twin parables of the mustard seed and the leaven, which follow the original parable. But the message is different. The economic circumstances of the poor farm worker and the rich merchant are very different, but their response is really the same. In the Old Testament, the treasure and the pearl are both symbols of wisdom. The disciple who had discovered the kingdom, the meaning of the Gospel message, is motivated to put all else aside for the sake of possessing it.

The final parable is also short, but, as to both message and form (an explanation is given), it belongs more with the parable of the wheat and the weeds. It continues the theme of the separation of the good and the bad "at the end of the age," the coming of the judgment, the fulfillment of the kingdom.

Notice how the hearers of the parables are themselves portrayed by, drawn into, a parable in verse 52. In contrast to the disciples in Mark's Gospel, Matthew has Jesus' closest followers answering "yes" to Jesus' question about understanding. He compliments them and assigns them a leadership role in the kingdom.

Jesus Is Rejected at Nazareth
(Also Mark 6.1–6; Luke 4.16–30)

[53]When Jesus finished telling these parables, he left that place [54]and went back to his hometown. He taught in their synagogue, and those who heard him were amazed. "Where did he get such wisdom?" they asked. "And what about his miracles? [55]Isn't he the carpenter's son? Isn't Mary his mother, and aren't James, Joseph, Simon, and Judas his brothers? [56]Aren't all his sisters living here? Where did he get all this?" [57]And so they rejected him. Jesus said to them: "A prophet is respected everywhere except in his hometown and by his own family." [58]He did not perform many miracles there because they did not have faith.

The Death of John the Baptist
(Also Mark 6.14–29; Luke 9.7–9)

14 It was at that time that Herod, the ruler of Galilee, heard about Jesus. [2]"He is

really John the Baptist who has come back to life," he told his officials. "That is why these powers are at work in him."

³For Herod had ordered John's arrest, and had him tied up and put in prison. He did this because of Herodias, his brother Philip's wife. ⁴John the Baptist kept telling Herod, "It isn't right for you to marry her!" ⁵Herod wanted to kill him, but he was afraid of the Jewish people, because they considered John to be a prophet.

⁶On Herod's birthday the daughter of Herodias danced in front of the whole group. Herod was so pleased ⁷that he promised her: "I swear that I will give you anything you ask for!" ⁸At her mother's suggestion she asked him, "Give me right here the head of John the Baptist on a plate!" ⁹The king was sad, but because of the promise he had made in front of all his guests he gave orders that her wish be granted. ¹⁰So he had John beheaded in prison. ¹¹The head was brought in on a plate and given to the girl, who took it to her mother. ¹²John's disciples came, got his body, and buried it; then they went and told Jesus.

Peter and the Church

The narrative of book four extends from 13:54 to 17:27. The conflict between Jesus and the Jewish leaders heightens, as Jesus rejects their teaching authority and bestows the right to interpret his teaching on Peter and the Church. "Peter" and "the Church" are key themes of this book, which ends significantly with the discourse on Church life and order. The union of Christ and his Church comes out strongly in book four.

The rejection of Jesus by Israel is summarized in miniature by his rejection at Nazareth (13:54–58). The townspeople marvel at Jesus' teaching and miracles. Yet these do not produce faith, because the Nazareans feel they know Jesus' lowly origins perfectly and so are confident that he could not be someone special. The question, "Is not he the son of the carpenter?" betrays their ignorance that Jesus, born of the virgin, is actually the Son of God. Like all the prophets before him, Jesus faces rejection by his people. He responds to their unbelief with a restriction of his miraculous activity. The theme of the rejection of the prophet is continued by the story of the death of the Baptist (14:1–12). The fate of John at the hands of the murderous King Herod foretells the fate of Jesus, the final prophet.

Jesus Feeds Five Thousand
(Also Mark 6.30–44; Luke 9.10–17; John 6.1–14)

[13]When Jesus heard the news, he left that place in a boat and went to a lonely place by himself. The people heard about it, left their towns, and followed him by land. [14]Jesus got out of the boat, and when he saw the large crowd his heart was filled with pity for them, and he healed their sick.

[15]That evening his disciples came to him and said, "It is already very late, and this is a lonely place. Send the people away and let them go to the villages and buy food for themselves." [16]"They don't have to leave," answered Jesus. "You yourselves give them something to eat." [17]"All we have here are five loaves and two fish," they replied. [18]"Bring them here to me," Jesus said, [19]He ordered the people to sit down on the grass; then he took the five loaves and the two fish, looked up to heaven, and gave thanks to God. He broke the

loaves and gave them to the disciples, and the disciples gave them to the people. ²⁰Everyone ate and had enough. Then the disciples took up twelve baskets full of what was left over. ²¹The number of men who ate was about five thousand, not counting the women and children.

Jesus Feeds Five Thousand

For the moment, Jesus withdraws before the evil king. But the crowds which follow him allow him to reveal himself as the genuine shepherd-ruler of Israel, who heals and nourishes his flock (14:13–21). As Moses and Elijah fed their hungry followers (Exodus 16; 2 Kings 4:42–44), so Jesus feeds the crowd of five thousand ''in the desert.'' Matthew stresses the sovereign control of Jesus over the situation, while not ignoring the role of the disciples as mediators of Christ's gift of bread. The story obviously looks forward to the Christian Eucharist and the heavenly banquet. Notice, by the way, how many passages in book four will mention the word ''bread'' or ''loaves.'' The bread symbol is a key theme of book four. It symbolizes the gift of Jesus in his Word and in his Eucharist.

Jesus Walks on the Water
(Also Mark 6.45–52; John 6.15–21)

²²Then Jesus made the disciples get into the boat and go ahead of him to the other side of the lake, while he sent the people away. ²³After sending the people away, he went up a hill by himself to pray. When evening came, Jesus was there alone; ²⁴by this time the boat was far out in the lake, tossed about by the waves, for the wind was blowing against it. ²⁵Between three and six o'clock in the morning Jesus came to them, walking on the water. ²⁶When

the disciples saw him walking on the water they were terrified. "It's a ghost!" they said, and screamed with fear. ²⁷Jesus spoke to them at once. "Courage!" he said. "It is I. Don't be afraid!" ²⁸Then Peter spoke up. "Lord," he said, "if it is really you, order me to come out on the water to you." ²⁹"Come!" answered Jesus. So Peter got out of the boat and started walking on the water to Jesus. ³⁰When he noticed the wind, however, he was afraid, and started to sink down in the water. "Save me, Lord!" he cried. ³¹At once Jesus reached out and grabbed him and said, "How little faith you have! Why did you doubt?" ³²They both got back into the boat, and the wind died down. ³³The disciples in the boat worshiped Jesus. "Truly you are the Son of God!" they exclaimed.

³⁴They crossed the lake and came to land at Gennesaret, ³⁵where the people recognized Jesus. So they sent for the sick people in all the surrounding country and brought them to Jesus. ³⁶They begged him to let the sick at least touch the edge of his cloak; and all who touched it were made well.

Jesus' walking on the water (14:22–33) symbolizes the aid Jesus brings to his Church as she is buffeted by the forces of chaos and death in the night of this world. Jesus bestrides the waters of chaos as does God or Wisdom in the Old Testament and speaks the divine "It is I!" At this point Matthew inserts the story of Peter attempting to walk on water, sinking because of fear, and being saved by the outstretched hand of the Lord. Jesus rebukes Peter's "little faith" and "doubt" that is the panic and hesitation which hounds the believer when faced with danger.

The Teaching of the Ancestors
(Also Mark 7.1–13)

15 Then some Pharisees and teachers of the Law came to Jesus from Jerusalem and asked him: ²"Why is it that your disciples disobey the teaching handed down by our ancestors? They don't wash their hands in the proper way before they eat!" ³Jesus answered: "And why do you disobey God's command and follow your own teaching? ⁴For God said, 'Honor your father and mother,' and 'Anyone who says bad things about his father or mother must be put to death.' ⁵But you teach that if a person has something he could use to help his father or mother, but says, 'This belongs to God,' ⁶he does not need to honor his father. This is how you disregard God's word to follow your own teaching. ⁷You hypocrites! How right Isaiah was when he prophesied about you!

⁸"These people, says God, honor me with their words,
But their heart is really far away from me.
⁹It is no use for them to worship me,
Because they teach man-made commandments as though they were God's rules!' "

¹⁰Then Jesus called the crowd to him and said to them: "Listen, and understand! ¹¹It is not what goes into a person's mouth that makes him unclean; rather, what comes out of it makes him unclean."

¹²Then the disciples came to him and said, "Do you know that the Pharisees had their feelings hurt by what you said?" ¹³"Every plant which my Father in heaven did not plant will be pulled up," answered Jesus. ¹⁴"Don't worry about them! They are blind leaders; and when

one blind man leads another, both fall in the ditch." [15]Peter spoke up, "Tell us what this parable means." [16]Jesus said to them: "You are still no more intelligent than the others. [17]Don't you understand? Anything that goes into a person's mouth goes into his stomach and then on out of the body. [18]But the things that come out of the mouth come from the heart; such things make a man unclean. [19]For from his heart come the evil ideas which lead him to kill, commit adultery, and do other immoral things; to rob, lie, and slander others. [20]These are the things that make a man unclean. But to eat without washing your hands as they say you should— this does not make a man unclean."

The Son of God shows his authority over oral tradition and written law in the next section (15:1–20). The Pharisees attack Jesus' disciples (that is, the Church) for transgressing their oral traditions about washing hands before eating. Jesus counters by asking why the Pharisees, through a legal loophole, transgress God's commandment about honoring father and mother. Such inversion of priorities and values is hypocrisy and idolatry. Jesus then dares to reject not only unwritten customs but even the food laws embedded in the Pentateuch. Defilement comes not from ritually unclean food but from immoral decisions and acts proceeding from man's heart. The disciples are frightened by this open cancellation of a part of Scripture, but Jesus replies that pharisaic Judaism (which is the adversary of Matthew's Church) has not been "planted" or established by the Father. The break between Judaism and Matthew's Church peeks through here. In rejecting ritual laws and customs, the Church desires to emphasize all the more strenuously the basic moral obligations enjoined in the ten commandments.

A Woman's Faith
(Also Mark 7.24–30)

[21]Jesus left that place and went off to the territory near the cities of Tyre and Sidon. [22]A Canaanite woman who lived in that region came to him. "Son of David, sir!" she cried. "Have mercy on me! My daughter has a demon and is in a terrible condition." [23]But Jesus did not say a word to her. His disciples came to him and begged him, "Send her away! She is following us and making all this noise!" [24]Then Jesus replied, "I have been sent only to the lost sheep of the people of Israel." [25]At this the woman came and fell at his feet. "Help me, sir!" she said. [26]Jesus answered, "It isn't right to take the children's food and throw it to the dogs." [27]"That is true, sir," she answered; "but even the dogs eat the leftovers that fall from their masters' table." [28]So Jesus answered her: "You are a woman of great faith! What you want will be done for you." And at that very moment her daughter was healed.

Jesus Heals Many People

[29]Jesus left that place and went along by Lake Galilee. He climbed a hill and sat down. [30]Large crowds came to him, bringing with them the lame, the blind, the crippled, the dumb, and many other sick people, whom they placed at Jesus' feet; and he healed them. [31]The people were amazed as they saw the dumb speaking, the crippled whole, the lame walking, and the blind seeing; and they praised the God of Israel.

[32]Jesus called his disciples to him and said: "I feel sorry for these people, because they have

been with me for three days and now have nothing to eat. I don't want to send them away without feeding them, because they might faint on their way home." [33]The disciples asked him, "Where will we find enough food in this desert to feed this crowd?" [34]"How much bread do you have?" Jesus asked. "Seven loaves," they answered, "and a few small fish." [35]So Jesus ordered the crowd to sit down on the ground. [36]Then he took the seven loaves and the fish, gave thanks to God, broke them and gave them to the disciples, and the disciples gave them to the people. [37]They all ate and had enough. The disciples took up seven baskets full of pieces left over. [38]The number of men who ate was four thousand, not counting the women and children.

[39]Then Jesus sent the people away, got into a boat, and went to the territory of Magadan.

Jesus thus destroys one of the great barriers separating Jews and gentiles. This destruction of barriers is dramatized in his encounter with the Canaanite woman (15:21–28)—one of the few instances in which Jesus has contact with gentiles in Matthew's Gospel. The woman shows her faith by acknowledging Jesus as her Lord and as Israel's Messiah. Jesus at first uses his exclusive mission to Israel as a reason for ignoring the woman's plea. But she cannot be put off, even by an apparent insult. Faith and humble prayer, plus a sense of humor, win the day. The woman reaffirms the special place of Israel. Yet, by her faith, she prefigures the future admission of gentiles into the Church. In 15:29–39, Matthew summarizes for the last time the bright side of Jesus' Galilean ministry: the sick are healed and a crowd of four thousand is fed.

■ Reflection

Are there any instances in which our Church shows itself to be as hostile to outsiders as the Judaism of Jesus' time?

The Demand for a Miracle
(Also Mark 8.11–13; Luke 12.54–56)

16 Some Pharisees and Sadducees came to Jesus. They wanted to trap him, so they asked him to perform a miracle for them, to show God's approval. ²But Jesus answered: "When the sun is setting you say, 'We are going to have fine weather, because the sky is red.' ³And early in the morning you say, 'It is going to rain, because the sky is red and dark.' You can predict the weather by looking at the sky; but you cannot interpret the signs concerning these times! ⁴How evil and godless are the people of this day!" Jesus added. "You ask me for a miracle? No! The only miracle you will be given is the miracle of Jonah." So he left them and went away.

⁵When the disciples crossed over to the other side of the lake, they forgot to take any bread. ⁶Jesus said to them, "Look out, and be on your guard against the yeast of the Pharisees and Sadducees." ⁷They started discussing among themselves: "He says this because we didn't bring any bread." ⁸Jesus knew what they were saying, so he asked them: "Why are you discussing among yourselves about not having any bread? How little faith you have! ⁹Don't you understand yet? Don't you remember when I broke the five loaves for the five thousand men? How many baskets did you fill? ¹⁰And what about the seven loaves for the four thousand men? How many baskets did

you fill? ¹¹How is it that you don't understand that I was not talking to you about bread? Guard yourselves from the yeast of the Pharisees and Sadducees!" ¹²Then the disciples understood that he was not telling them to guard themselves from the yeast used in bread, but from the teaching of the Pharisees and Sadducees.

In 16:1–12, the Pharisees and Sadducees, symbolizing the united front of Judaism, again express their unbelief by demanding a sign on their own terms. Jesus again refuses to give them any sign except his death-resurrection (see 12:38–40). Jesus then rebukes his disciples for their lack of trust in Jesus' power, in that they are still worried about material needs. More importantly, Jesus warns them to beware of the leaven, that is, the corrupting doctrine of the Jewish leaders. Jesus thus rejects the Jewish "magisterium" or teaching authority just before he confers that authority on Peter.

Peter's Declaration About Jesus
(Also Mark 8.27–30; Luke 9.18–21)

¹³Jesus went to the territory near the town of Caesarea Philippi, where he asked his disciples, "Who do men say the Son of Man is?" ¹⁴"Some say John the Baptist," they answered. "Others say Elijah, while others say Jeremiah or some other prophet." ¹⁵"What about you?" he asked them. "Who do you say I am?" ¹⁶Simon Peter answered, "You are the Messiah, the Son of the living God." ¹⁷"Simon, son of John, you are happy indeed!" answered Jesus. "For this truth did not come to you from any human being, but it was given to you directly by my Father in heaven. ¹⁸And so I tell you: you are a rock, Peter, and on this rock I

will build my church. Not even death will ever be able to overcome it. [19]I will give you the keys of the Kingdom of heaven: what you prohibit on earth will be prohibited in heaven; what you permit on earth will be permitted in heaven." [20]Then Jesus ordered his disciples that they were not to tell anyone that he was the Messiah.

Jesus Speaks About His Suffering and Death
(Also Mark 8.31—9.1; Luke 9.22—27)

[21]From that time on Jesus began to say plainly to his disciples: "I must go to Jerusalem and suffer much from the elders, the chief priests, and the teachers of the Law. I will be put to death, and on the third day I will be raised to life." [22]Peter took him aside and began to rebuke him. "God forbid it, Lord!" he said. "This must never happen to you!" [23]Jesus turned around and said to Peter: "Get away from me, Satan! You are an obstacle in my way, for these thoughts of yours are men's thoughts, not God's!"

[24]Then Jesus said to his disciples: "If anyone wants to come with me, he must forget himself, carry his cross, and follow me. [25]For the man who wants to save his own life will lose it; but the man who loses his life for my sake will find it. [26]Will a man gain anything if he wins the whole world but loses his life? Of course not! There is nothing a man can give to regain his life. [27]For the Son of Man is about to come in the glory of his Father with his angels, and then he will repay everyone according to his deeds. [28]Remember this! There are some here who will not die until they have seen the Son of Man come as King."

Peter's Confession

Matthew's great concern—Christ and his Church—is played out to the full in the scene at Caesarea Philippi (16:13–28). Rejecting the insufficient answers of "public opinion," Jesus directly challenges the disciples to define him adequately. Peter the spokesman proclaims that Jesus the Son of Man (verse 13) is the longed-for Messiah of Israel and, even more, the Son of the living God. As soon as Simon confers these titles on Jesus, Jesus reciprocates by conferring a title and office on Simon. Simon has been graced with a special revelation from Jesus' Father, and so Simon receives from Jesus the title *Peter,* which means " the Rock." He is to be the firm, bedrock foundation on which Jesus will build his holy assembly, the eschatological people of God, in other words, "my Church." Death itself will not be able to overcome the unshakable structure Jesus erects on Peter, who is invested with the powers of major-domo ("the power of the keys") in the palace of the Messiah-King Jesus (see Isaiah 22:15–25). Peter will receive the power to bind and loose, that is, to decide for the whole Church what actions are in keeping or not in keeping with the teachings of Jesus. The decisions of the "chief rabbi" Peter will be confirmed by God at the final judgment.

Jesus orders the disciples to tell no one about his Messiahship, since "Messiah" could easily lead to nationalistic dreams of glory. To counter any such misconception, Jesus utters the first prediction of his passion, death, and resurrection. While Peter was happy to confess Jesus as Messiah and Son of God, he rebels against this revelation of Jesus as the suffering Son of Man. Jesus harshly rebukes Peter, who, like Satan in 4:10, tries to turn Jesus away from the path of suffering. The Rock turns into a stumbling stone, a scandal, for

Jesus. Jesus insists that the cross is the necessary price of glory, both for himself and his disciples. The believer must accept the paradox of earthly loss for the sake of eternal gain.

The Transfiguration
(Also Mark 9.2–13; Luke 9.28–36)

17 Six days later Jesus took with him Peter, and the brothers James and John, and led them up a high mountain by themselves. [2]As they looked on, a change came over him: his face became as bright as the sun, and his clothes as white as light. [3]Then the three disciples saw Moses and Elijah talking with Jesus. [4]So Peter spoke up and said to Jesus, "Lord, it is a good thing that we are here; if you wish, I will make three tents here, one for you, one for Moses, and one for Elijah." [5]While he was talking, a shining cloud came over them and a voice said from the cloud: "This is my own dear Son, with whom I am well pleased—listen to him!" [6]When the disciples heard the voice they were so terrified that they threw themselves face down to the ground. [7]Jesus came to them and touched them. "Get up," he said. "Don't be afraid!" [8]So they looked up and saw no one else except Jesus.

[9]As they came down the mountain Jesus ordered them: "Don't tell anyone about this vision you have seen until the Son of Man has been raised from death." [10]Then the disciples asked Jesus, "Why do the teachers of the Law say that Elijah has to come first?" [11]"Elijah does indeed come first," answered Jesus, "and he will get everything ready. [12]But I tell you this: Elijah has already come and people did not recognize him, but treated him just as they

pleased. In the same way the Son of Man will also be mistreated by them." [13]Then the disciples understood that he was talking to them about John the Baptist.

[14]When they returned to the crowd, a man came to Jesus, knelt before him, [15]and said: "Sir, have mercy on my son! He is an epileptic and has such terrible fits that he often falls in the fire or in the water. [16]I brought him to your disciples, but they could not heal him." [17]Jesus answered: "How unbelieving and wrong you people are! How long must I stay with you? How long do I have to put up with you? Bring the boy here to me!" [18]Jesus commanded the demon and it went out, so that the boy was healed at that very moment.

[19]Then the disciples came to Jesus in private and asked him, "Why couldn't we drive the demon out?" [20]"It was because you do not have enough faith," answered Jesus. "Remember this! If you have faith as big as a mustard seed, you can say to this hill, 'Go from here to there!' and it will go. You could do anything! [[21]But only prayer and fasting can drive this kind out; nothing else can.]"

The Transfiguration

The transfiguration (17:1–13) confirms Peter's profession of faith and also develops the connection between the titles *Son of God* and *Son of Man*. The radiant transformation of Jesus' appearance shows that Jesus is truly a heavenly being. Moses and Elijah, the law and the prophets, point to the glory of this Son of Man. Since Peter fails to understand the vision, God himself reveals its meaning: Jesus is the beloved Son—thus repeating the revelation at the baptism (3:17). The disciples are to listen to him as the Israelites were commanded to listen to Moses (Deuteronomy 18:15). As they descend from the mount, Jesus hammers home the truth that, just as the Baptist suffered the death of a martyred prophet at the hands of an unbelieving Israel, so too must he.

The struggle between belief and unbelief is dramatized in the story of the epileptic boy (17:14–20). Jesus rebukes the unbelief of Israel, rewards the imperfect but sincere faith of the father by curing his epileptic child, and then informs the disciples that their "littleness of faith" prevented them from healing the boy. In Matthew, the disciples believe Jesus and understand what he says; but they do not trust God fully.

Jesus Speaks Again About His Death
(Also Mark 9.30–32; Luke 9.43b–45)

²²When the disciples all came together in Galilee, Jesus said to them: "The Son of Man is about to be handed over to men ²³who will kill him; but on the third day he will be raised to life." The disciples became very sad.

²⁴When Jesus and his disciples came to Capernaum, the collectors of the Temple tax came to Peter and asked, "Does your teacher pay the Temple tax?" ²⁵"Of course," Peter answered. When Peter went into the house, Jesus spoke up first: "Simon, what is your opinion? Who pays duties or taxes to the kings of this world? The citizens of the country or the foreigners?" ²⁶"The foreigners," answered Peter. "Well, then," replied Jesus, "that means that the citizens don't have to pay. ²⁷But we don't want to offend these people. So go to the lake and drop in a line; pull up the first fish you hook, and in its mouth you will find a coin worth enough for my Temple tax and yours; take it and pay them our taxes."

The Journey Begins

As Jesus gathers his disciples for the journey to Jerusalem, he again discourages any dreams of glory by issuing the second prediction of his passion (17:22–23). This is followed by a concluding narrative involving Jesus and Peter (17:24–27). The collectors of the Temple tax automatically direct their question about Jesus' decision to pay or not to pay the tax to Peter. Peter impetuously says yes. Jesus then uses a parable to show Peter that Jesus the Son, and indeed all the sons in God's kingdom, are exempt from the Temple tax levied upon mere subjects. Yet Jesus mercifully waives his exemption in order not to offend anyone, even his enemies. Jesus provides for payment of the tax—but only for Peter and himself. The bond between the Messiah and the foundation-stone of his Church is thus emphasized for the final time in the narrative of book four.

Who Is the Greatest?
(Also Mark 9.33–37; Luke 9.46–48)

18 At that moment the disciples came to Jesus, asking, "Who is the greatest in the Kingdom of heaven?" ²Jesus called a child, had him stand in front of them, ³and said: "Remember this! Unless you change and become like children, you will never enter the Kingdom of heaven. ⁴The greatest in the Kingdom of heaven is the one who humbles himself and becomes like this child. ⁵And the person who welcomes in my name one such child as this, welcomes me."

⁶"As for these little ones who believe in me—it would be better for a man to have a large millstone tied around his neck and be drowned in the deep sea, than for him to cause one of them to turn away from me. ⁷How

terrible for the world that there are things that make people turn away! Such things will always happen—but how terrible for the one who causes them!

8"If your hand or your foot makes you turn away, cut it off and throw it away! It is better for you to enter life without a hand or foot than to keep both hands and feet and be thrown into the eternal fire. 9And if your eye makes you turn away, take it out and throw it away! It is better for you to enter life with only one eye than to keep both eyes and be thrown into the fire of hell."

10"See that you don't despise any of these little ones. Their angels in heaven, I tell you, are always in the presence of my Father in heaven. [11For the Son of Man came to save the lost.]

12"What do you think? What will a man do who has one hundred sheep and one of them gets lost? He will leave the other ninety-nine grazing on the hillside and go to look for the lost sheep. 13When he finds it, I tell you, he feels far happier over this one sheep than over the ninety-nine that did not get lost. 14In just the same way your Father in heaven does not want any of these little ones to be lost."

15"If your brother sins against you, go to him and show him his fault. But do it privately, just between yourselves. If he listens to you, you have won your brother back. 16But if he will not listen to you, take one or two other persons with you, so that 'every accusation may be upheld by the testimony of two or three witnesses,' as the scripture says. 17But if he will not listen to them, then tell the whole thing to the church. And then, if he will not listen to the church, treat him as though he were a foreigner or a tax collector."

¹⁸"And so I tell all of you: what you prohibit on earth will be prohibited in heaven; what you permit on earth will be permitted in heaven.

¹⁹"And I tell you more: whenever two of you on earth agree about anything you pray for, it will be done for you by my Father in heaven. ²⁰For where two or three come together in my name, I am there with them."

Chapter 18 can be divided into two main sections: pastoral concern for children and the little ones (18:1–14) and pastoral concern for the brother who sins (18:15–35). Each section may be further divided into subsections: verses 1–5 treat of children, while verses 6–14 treat of the little ones; verses 15–20 treat of Church discipline in the case of the brother who sins, while verses 21–35 treat of the obligation to forgive the brother who sins. Notice how each major section ends with a parable.

Verses 1–5 begin with the question of greatness in the kingdom—both in its last stage after the final coming of Jesus as judge and in its preliminary stage in the Church. To answer by a parable in action, Jesus summons a child and makes this no-account person, without rights and privileges in the ancient world, the model of true greatness in the kingdom. The true sons of the kingdom, who preserve a child-like reliance upon the Father, are those who have access to the kingdom and greatness in it.

Verses 6–14 shift the topic to "the little ones" that is to say, the apparently "unimportant" members of the community who can easily wander off because they are not receiving careful attention. The lack of care can take the form either of positively causing the little ones to fall into sin (verses 6–9) or simply of not going after these sheep when they stray (verses 10–14).

Besides those who stray from the community through weakness, there are those who sin and yet remain in the community. Verses 15–20 take up the problem of how these sinful brothers are to be corrected. The first steps should be private, to safeguard everyone's honor in the family. When resistance is met, further witnesses are called in (see Deuteronomy 19:15). When all private correction fails , the local church is convened. If the sinner refuses to obey the whole Church, he is cast out and loses his membership in the people of God. While binding and loosing in 16:19 referred to Peter's power to teach, the phrase in 18:18 is rather concerned with the local church's power to excommunicate or to admit to the Church. Such decisions are ratified by the Father in heaven and made possible by the presence of Jesus in the midst of the believers.

The Unforgiving Servant

[21]Then Peter came to Jesus and asked, "Lord, how many times can my brother sin against me and I have to forgive him? Seven times?" [22]"No, not seven times," answered Jesus, "but seventy times seven. [23]Because the Kingdom of heaven is like a king who decided to check on his servants' accounts. [24]He had just begun to do so when one of them was brought in who owed him millions of dollars. [25]He did not have enough to pay his debt, so his master ordered him to be sold as a slave, with his wife and his children and all that he had, in order to pay the debt. [26]The servant fell on his knees before his master. 'Be patient with me,' he begged, 'and I will pay you everything!'

[27]The master felt sorry for him, so he forgave him the debt and let him go.

[28]"The man went out and met one of his fellow servants who owed him a few dollars. He grabbed him and started choking him. 'Pay back what you owe me!' he said. [29]His fellow servant fell down and begged him, 'Be patient with me and I will pay you back!' [30]But he would not; instead, he had him thrown into jail until he should pay the debt. [31]When the other servants saw what had happened, they were very upset, and went to their master and told him everything. [32]So the master called the servant in. 'You worthless slave!' he said. 'I forgave you the whole amount you owed me, just because you asked me to. [33]You should have had mercy on your fellow servant, just as I had mercy on you.' [34]The master was very angry, and he sent the servant to jail to be punished until he should pay back the whole amount." [35]And Jesus concluded, "That is how my Father in heaven will treat you if you do not forgive your brother, every one of you, from your heart."

Forgiveness

But the last word on Church discipline must be mercy. In the family of the Church, forgiveness must be given as often as it is sincerely requested. The parable points out that we have all been forgiven an infinite debt by our King and Father, and so none of us has the right to withhold forgiveness from our brothers and sisters. None of us can earn God's forgiveness. But we can lose it by refusing to give it away to others as freely as we have received it. Forgive—this is Jesus' final word in his discourse on life in the Church and in book four of the ministry.

■ Reflection

How are disputes among members of the Church handled today? Do we continue to observe the Gospel tradition?

■ Discussion

1. Is the Word of God in the Gospels limited to what Jesus actually said? How important is it for us to know which are the actual words of the historical Jesus?

2. Were any of the lessons taught by Jesus in the parables new teachings for the Israelites?

3. What contemporary images might be used to form teaching stories for twentieth-century men and women who are concerned about religious tastes?

4. What aspects of our understanding of the papacy can be derived from Matthew's description of the relationship between Jesus and Peter?

5. What understanding of Church can be derived from Matthew's Gospel to this point? Is it an understanding commonly held by Christians today?

■ Prayer and Meditation

"You are all I want, O LORD;
    I promise to keep your laws. . . .
The law that you gave means more to me
    than all the money in the world. . . .
Let your constant love comfort me,
    as you have promised to me, your servant. . . .
I love your commands more than gold,
    more than the finest gold. . . .
Those who love your laws have perfect security,
    and there is nothing that can make them fall."

From Psalm 119

The Passion and Death _____ Matthew 19:1—27:66

In the last of the five books of the public ministry, Jesus the Son leads his fledgling Church up to Jerusalem to face and confound the leaders of Judaism for the last time. Having pronounced judgment on the teachers of Israel, Jesus prophesies the tribulations which will lead to the last judgment, a judgment which touches the Church as well as the world.

Jesus Teaches About Divorce
(Also Mark 10.1–12)

19 When Jesus finished saying these things, he left Galilee and went back to the territory of Judea, on the other side of the Jordan river. ²Large crowds followed him, and he healed them there.

³Some Pharisees came to him and tried to trap him by asking, "Does our Law allow a man to divorce his wife for any and every reason?" ⁴Jesus answered: "Haven't you read this scripture? 'In the beginning the Creator made them male and female', ⁵and God said, 'For this reason a man will leave his father and mother and unite with his wife, and the two will become one.' ⁶So they are no longer two, but one. Man must not separate, then, what God has

115

joined together." ⁷The Pharisees asked him, "Why, then, did Moses give the commandment for a man to give his wife a divorce notice and send her away?" ⁸Jesus answered: "Moses gave you permission to divorce your wives because you are so hard to teach. But it was not this way at the time of creation. ⁹I tell you, then, that any man who divorces his wife, and she has not been unfaithful, commits adultery if he marries some other woman."

¹⁰His disciples said to him, "If this is the way it is between a man and his wife, it is better not to marry." ¹¹Jesus answered: "This teaching does not apply to everyone, but only to those to whom God has given it. ¹²For there are different reasons why men cannot marry: some, because they were born that way; others, because men made them that way; and others do not marry because of the Kingdom of heaven. Let him who can do it accept this teaching."

¹³Some people brought children to Jesus for him to place his hands on them and pray, but the disciples scolded those people. ¹⁴Jesus said, "Let the children come to me, and do not stop them, because the Kingdom of heaven belongs to such as these." ¹⁵He placed his hands on them and left.

The Rich Young Man
(Also Mark 10.17–31; Luke 18.18–30)

¹⁶Once a man came to Jesus. "Teacher," he asked, "what good thing must I do to receive eternal life?" ¹⁷"Why do you ask me concerning what is good?" answered Jesus. "There is only One who is good. Keep the commandments if you want to enter life." ¹⁸"What command-

ments?'' he asked. Jesus answered; "Do not murder; do not commit adultery; do not steal; do not lie; [19]honor your father and mother; and love your neighbor as yourself" [20]"I have obeyed all these commandments," the young man replied. "What else do I need to do?" [21]Jesus said to him, "If you want to be perfect, go and sell all you have and give the money to the poor, and you will have riches in heaven; then come and follow me." [22]When the young man heard this he went away sad, because he was very rich.

[23]Jesus then said to his disciples: "It will be very hard, I tell you, for a rich man to enter the Kingdom of heaven. [24]I tell you something else: it is much harder for a rich man to enter the Kingdom of God than for a camel to go through the eye of a needle." [25]When the disciples heard this they were completely amazed. "Who can be saved, then?" they asked. [26]Jesus looked straight at them and answered, "This is impossible for men; but for God everything is possible."

Teachings on Vocation

On the way up to Jerusalem and the cross, the Messiah teaches the members of his Church their duties in their various states of life—life lived under the cross. Married people and celibates are the first addressed (19:1–12). With sovereign power over the law, Jesus rejects divorce, although it was allowed by Deuteronomy. The apparent exception, "except for immorality," probably refers to incestuous unions. Celibacy is a special gift which makes sense for those who undertake it because of the coming of the kingdom which has already invaded their lives. Children likewise have their place in the kingdom and serve as an example for all who are called to admit their dependence on the Father (19:13–15). The case of the rich is more problematic (19:16–26). The rich young man cannot measure up to the challenge to leave all things to follow Jesus. Yet Jesus affirms that even the rich can be saved, thanks to God's omnipotent grace.

²⁷Then Peter spoke up. "Look," he said, "we have left everything and followed you. What will we have?" ²⁸Jesus said to them: "I tell you this: when the Son of Man sits on his glorious throne in the New Age, then you twelve followers of mine will also sit on thrones, to judge the twelve tribes of Israel. ²⁹And every one who has left houses or brothers or sisters or father or mother or children or fields for my sake, will receive a hundred times more, and will be given eternal life. ³⁰But many who now are first will be last, and many who now are last will be first."

The Workers in the Vineyard

20 "The Kingdom of heaven is like the owner of a vineyard who went out early in the morning to hire some men to work in his vineyard. ²He agreed to pay them the regular wage, a silver coin a day, and sent them to work in his vineyard. ³He went out again to the marketplace at nine o'clock and saw some men standing there doing nothing, ⁴so he told them, 'You also go to work in the vineyard, and I will pay you a fair wage.' ⁵So they went. Then at twelve o'clock and again at three o'clock he did the same thing. ⁶It was nearly five o'clock when he went to the marketplace and saw some other men still standing there. 'Why are you wasting the whole day here doing nothing?' he asked them. [7]'It is because no one hired us,' they answered. 'Well, then, you also go to work in the vineyard,' he told them.

[8]"When evening came, the owner told his foreman, 'Call the workers and pay them their wages, starting with those who were hired last, and ending with those who were hired first.' [9]The men who had begun to work at five o'clock were paid a silver coin each. [10]So when the men who were the first to be hired came to be paid, they thought they would get more—but they too were given a silver coin each. [11]They took their money and started grumbling against the employer. [12]'These men who were hired last worked only one hour,' they said, 'while we put up with a whole day's work in the hot sun—yet you paid them the same as you paid us!' [13]'Listen, friend,' the owner answered one of them. 'I have not cheated you. After all, you agreed to do a day's work for a silver coin. [14]Now, take your pay and go home. I want to give this man who was hired last as much as I have given you. [15]Don't I have the right to do as I wish with my own money? Or are you jealous simply because I am generous?' " [16]And Jesus added, "So those who are last will be first, and those who are first will be last."

[17]As Jesus was going up to Jerusalem he took the twelve disciples aside and spoke to them privately, as they walked along. [18]"Listen," he told them, "we are going up to Jerusalem, where the Son of Man will be handed over to the chief priests and the teachers of the Law. They will condemn him to death [19]and then hand him over to the Gentiles, who will make fun of him, whip him, and nail him to the cross; and on the third day he will be raised to life."

A Mother's Request
(Also Mark 10.35-45)

[20]Then the mother of Zebedee's sons came to Jesus with her sons, bowed before him, and asked him for a favor. [21]"What do you want?" Jesus asked her. She answered, "Promise that these two sons of mine will sit at your right and your left when you are King." [22]"You don't know what you are asking for," Jesus answered them, "Can you drink the cup that I am about to drink?" "We can," they answered, [23]"You will indeed drink from my cup," Jesus told them, "but I do not have the right to choose who will sit at my right and my left. These places belong to those for whom my Father has prepared them."

[24]When the other ten disciples heard about this they became angry with the two brothers. [25]So Jesus called them all together to him and said: "You know that the rulers of the people have power over them, and the leaders rule over them. [26]This, however, is not the way it shall be among you. If one of you wants to be great, he must be the servant of the rest; [27]and if one of you wants to be first, he must be your slave—[28]like the Son of Man, who did not come to be served, but to serve and to give his life to redeem many people."

[29]As they were leaving Jericho a large crowd followed Jesus. [30]Two blind men who were sitting by the road heard that Jesus was passing by, so they began to shout, "Son of David! Have mercy on us, sir!" [31]The crowd scolded them and told them to be quiet. But they shouted, even more loudly, "Son of David! Have mercy on us, sir!" [32]Jesus stopped and called them. "What do you want me to do for you?" he asked them. [33]"Sir," they answered,

"we want you to open our eyes!" [34]Jesus had pity on them and touched their eyes; at once they were able to see, and they followed him.

Jesus promises the disciples who do leave all for him the reward of eternal life. Yet, as the parable of the laborers in the vineyard shows, the idea of reward must not lead them to think in terms of an ironclad legal claim on God (19:27—20:16). Dreams of rewards are blunted by the third prediction of the passion (20:17–19). When the mother of James and John ignores this straightforward warning by asking for the best seats in the kingdom for her sons, Jesus replies that they will certainly share his sufferings (20:20–28). Rewards, however, lie in the power of Jesus' Father. Turning the disciples' desires upside down, Jesus holds up his own service unto death as the ideal for all leaders in the Church. While the Twelve remain blind to the message of the cross in their lives, two blind men receive sight from Jesus (20:29–34). Their response is to "follow" Jesus on his way to the cross—precisely what the Twelve should be doing—with complete trust.

The Triumphant Entry into Jerusalem
(Also Mark 11.1–11; Luke 19.28–40; John 12.12–19)

21 As they approached Jerusalem, they came to Bethphage, at the Mount of Olives. There Jesus sent two of the disciples on ahead [2]with these instructions: "Go to the village there ahead of you, and at once you will find a donkey tied up and her colt with her. Untie them and bring them to me. [3]And if anyone says anything, tell him, 'The Master needs them'; and he will let them go at once."

⁴This happened to make come true what the prophet had said:

⁵"Tell the city of Zion:
Now your king is coming to you,
He is gentle and rides on a donkey,
He rides on a colt, the foal of a donkey."

⁶So the disciples went ahead and did what Jesus had told them to do: ⁷they brought the donkey and the colt, threw their cloaks over them, and Jesus got on. ⁸A great crowd of people spread their cloaks on the road, while others cut branches from the trees and spread them on the road. ⁹The crowds walking in front of Jesus and the crowds walking behind began to shout, "Praise to David's Son! God bless him who comes in the name of the Lord! Praise be to God!"

¹⁰When Jesus entered Jerusalem the whole city was thrown into an uproar. "Who is he?" the people asked. ¹¹"This is the prophet Jesus, from Nazareth of Galilee," the crowds answered.

¹²Jesus went into the Temple and drove out all those who bought and sold in the Temple; he overturned the tables of the money-changers and the stools of those who sold pigeons, ¹³and said to them: "It is written in the Scriptures that God said, 'My house will be called a house of prayer.' But you are making it a hideout for thieves!"

¹⁴The blind and the crippled came to him in the Temple and he healed them. ¹⁵The chief priests and the teachers of the Law became angry when they saw the wonderful things he was doing, and the children shouting and crying in the Temple, "Praise to David's Son!" ¹⁶So they said to Jesus, "Do you hear what they are saying?" "Indeed I do," answered Jesus.

"Haven't you ever read this scripture? 'You have trained children and babies to offer perfect praise' " [17]Jesus left them and went out of the city to Bethany, where he spent the night.

Jesus Curses the Fig Tree
(Also Mark 11.12–14,20–24)

[18]On his way back to the city, the next morning, Jesus was hungry. [19]He saw a fig tree by the side of the road and went to it, but found nothing on it except leaves. So he said to the tree, "You will never again bear fruit!" At once the fig tree dried up. [20]The disciples saw this and were astounded. "How did the fig tree dry up so quickly?" they asked. [21]"Remember this!" Jesus answered. "If you believe, and do not doubt, you will be able to do what I have done to this fig tree; not only this, you will even be able to say to this hill, 'Get up and throw yourself in the sea,' and it will. [22]If you believe, you will receive whatever you ask for in prayer."

Palm Sunday

Jesus' royal entry into Jerusalem (21:1–11) fulfills literally the hopes of the prophets for a peaceable king (see Isaiah 62:11; Zechariah 9:9). The coming of the prophet-king and son of David shakes the holy city to its foundation and prefigures his triumphant coming to his Church. The conflict between Israel, the old people of God, and the Church, the new people of God, is acted out by Jesus' cleansing of the Temple and his healing of the blind and the lame, who were barred from the Jerusalem Temple (21:12–17). The opposition of the chief priests and scribes portends the passion. Jesus' judgment on pharisaic Judaism—all leaves and no fruit—is dramatized by his cursing the barren fig tree (21:18–22).

The Question About Jesus' Authority
(Also Mark 11.27–33; Luke 20.1–8)

²³Jesus came back to the Temple; and as he taught, the chief priests and the Jewish elders came to him and asked, "What right do you have to do these things? Who gave you this right?" ²⁴Jesus answered them: "I will ask you just one question, and if you give me an answer I will tell you what right I have to do these things. ²⁵Where did John's right to baptize come from: from God or from man?" They started to argue among themselves: "What shall we say? If we answer, 'From God,' he will say to us, 'Why, then, did you not believe John?' ²⁶But if we say, 'From man,' we are afraid of what the people might do, because they are all convinced that John was a prophet." ²⁷So they answered Jesus, "We do not know." And he said to them, "Neither will I tell you, then, by what right I do these things."

The Parable of the Two Sons

²⁸"Now, what do you think? There was a man who had two sons. He went to the older one and said, 'Son, go work in the vineyard today.' ²⁹'I don't want to,' he answered, but later he changed his mind and went to the vineyard. ³⁰Then the father went to the other son and said the same thing. 'Yes, sir,' he answered, but he did not go. ³¹Which one of the two did what his father wanted?" "The older one," they answered. "And I tell you this," Jesus said to them. "The tax collectors and the

prostitutes are going into the Kingdom of God ahead of you. ³²For John the Baptist came to you showing you the right path to take, and you would not believe him; but the tax collectors and the prostitutes believed him. Even when you saw this you did not change your minds later on and believe him."

³³"Listen to another parable," Jesus said. "There was a landowner who planted a vineyard, put a fence around it, dug a hole for the winepress, and built a tower. Then he rented the vineyard to tenants and left home on a trip. ³⁴When the time came to harvest the grapes he sent his slaves to the tenants to receive his share. ³⁵The tenants grabbed his slaves, beat one, killed another, and stoned another. ³⁶Again the man sent other slaves, more than the first time, and the tenants treated them the same way. ³⁷Last of all he sent them his son. 'Surely they will respect my son,' he said. ³⁸But when the tenants saw the son they said to themselves, 'This is the owner's son. Come on, let us kill him, and we will get his property!' ³⁹So they grabbed him, threw him out of the vineyard, and killed him.

⁴⁰"Now, when the owner of the vineyard comes, what will he do to those tenants?" Jesus asked. ⁴¹"He will certainly kill those evil men," they answered, "and rent the vineyard out to other tenants, who will give him his share of the harvest at the right time." ⁴²Jesus said to them, "Haven't you ever read what the Scriptures say?

'The stone which the builders rejected
as worthless
Turned out to be the most important
stone.
This was done by the Lord,
How wonderful it is!'

43"And so I tell you," added Jesus, "the Kingdom of God will be taken away from you and be given to a people who will produce the proper fruits. [44Whoever falls on this stone will be broken to pieces; and if the stone falls on someone it will crush him to dust.]"

45The chief priests and the Pharisees heard Jesus' parables and knew that he was talking about them, 46so they tried to arrest him. But they were afraid of the crowds, who considered Jesus to be a prophet.

The Parable of the Wedding Feast
(Also Luke 14.15—24)

22 Jesus again used parables in talking to the people. 2"The Kingdom of heaven is like a king who prepared a wedding feast for his son. 3He sent his servants to tell the invited guests to come to the feast, but they did not want to come. 4So he sent other servants with the message: 'My feast is ready now; my steers and prize calves have been butchered, and everything is ready. Come to the wedding feast!' 5But the invited guests paid no attention and went about their business: one went to his farm, another to his store, 6while others grabbed the servants, beat them, and killed them. 7The king was very angry, and sent his soldiers and killed those murderers, and burned down their city. 8Then he called his servants. 'My wedding feast is ready,' he said, 'but the people I invited did not deserve it. 9Now go to the main streets and invite to the feast as many people as you find.' 10So the servants went out into the streets and gathered all the people they could find, good and bad alike; and the wedding hall was filled with people.

> [11]"The king went in to look at the guests and he saw a man who was not wearing wedding clothes. [12]'Friend, how did you get in here without wedding clothes?' the king asked him. But the man said nothing. [13]Then the king told the servants, 'Tie him up hand and foot and throw him outside in the dark. There he will cry and gnash his teeth.'" [14]And Jesus concluded, "For many are invited, but few are chosen."

The first public clash between the priests and Jesus over Jesus' authority (21:23–27) sets the stage for the parables, dispute stories, and woes which follow (chapters 21—23). Jesus shows that the leaders cannot even give clear teaching on such an important figure as the martyred Baptist. Jesus thus feels no obligation to submit his teaching authority to theirs. Matthew emphasizes Jesus' rejection of the Jewish leaders in three parables. The parable of the two sons rebukes the Jewish leaders for saying yes to God's will but not doing it, while religious outcasts responded favorably to the prophetic preaching of the Baptist (21:28–32). The parable of the evil tenants of the vineyard outlines the constant rejection which culminates in the murder of the Son and the destruction of Jerusalem (21:33–46). Significantly, Matthew adds to the Markan parable the idea that the kingdom of God will be given to another people (the Church). The parable of the royal wedding feast, with the appended parable of the wedding garment, carries the outline of salvation history up to the last judgment, a judgment which may condemn members of the Church as well as Israel (22:1–14).

The Question About Paying Taxes
(Also Mark 12.13—17; Luke 20.20—26)

¹⁵The Pharisees went off and made a plan to trap Jesus with questions. ¹⁶Then they sent some of their disciples and some members of Herod's party to Jesus. "Teacher," they said, "we know that you are an honest man: you teach the truth about God's will for man, without worrying about what people think, because you pay no attention to what a man seems to be. ¹⁷Tell us then, what do you think? Is it against our Law to pay taxes to the Roman Emperor, or not?" ¹⁸Jesus was aware of their evil plan, however, and so he said: "You impostors! Why are you trying to trap me? ¹⁹Show me the coin to pay the tax!" They brought him the coin, ²⁰and he asked them, "Whose face and name are these?" ²¹"The Emperor's," they answered. So Jesus said to them, "Well, then, pay to the Emperor what belongs to him, and pay to God what belongs to God." ²²When they heard this, they were filled with wonder; and they left him and went away.

²³That same day some Sadducees came to Jesus. (They are the ones who say that people will not rise from death.) ²⁴"Teacher," they said, "Moses taught: 'If a man who has no children dies, his brother must marry the widow so they can have children for the dead man.' ²⁵Now, there were seven brothers who used to live here. The oldest got married, and died without having children, so he left his widow to his brother. ²⁶The same thing happened to the second brother, to the third, and finally to all seven. ²⁷Last of all, the woman died. ²⁸Now, on the day when the dead are raised to life, whose wife will she be? All of them had married her!"

²⁹Jesus answered them: "How wrong you are! It is because you don't know the Scriptures or God's power. ³⁰For when the dead are raised to life they will be like the angels in heaven, and men and women will not marry. ³¹Now, about the dead being raised: haven't you ever read what God has told you? For he said, ³²'I am the God of Abraham, the God of Isaac, and the God of Jacob.' This means that he is the God of the living, not of the dead." ³³When the crowds heard this they were amazed at his teaching.

The Great Commandment
(Also Mark 12.28–34; Luke 10.25–28)

³⁴When the Pharisees heard that Jesus had silenced the Sadducees, they came together, ³⁵and one of them, a teacher of the Law, tried to trap him with a question. ³⁶"Teacher," he asked, "which is the greatest commandment in the Law?" ³⁷Jesus answered, " 'You must love the Lord your God with all your heart, and with all your soul, and with all your mind.' ³⁸This is the greatest and the most important commandment. ³⁹The second most important commandment is like it: 'You must love your neighbor as yourself.' ⁴⁰The whole Law of Moses and the teachings of the prophets depend on these two commandments."

⁴¹When the Pharisees gathered together, Jesus asked them: ⁴²"What do you think about the Messiah? Whose descendant is he?" "He is David's descendant," they answered. ⁴³"Why, then," Jesus asked, "did the Spirit inspire David to call him 'Lord'? For David said, ⁴⁴'The Lord said to my Lord: Sit here at my right side, Until I put your enemies under your feet.' ⁴⁵If,

then, David called him 'Lord,' how can the Messiah be David's descendant?" [46]No one was able to answer Jesus a single word, and from that day on no one dared ask him any more questions.

Matthew now moves back to Mark's collection of four dispute stories, which Matthew used to underline Jesus' rejection of the teaching authority of the Jewish leaders (22:15–46). The Pharisees and Herodians fail to ensnare Jesus by asking about the legitimacy of paying taxes to Caesar (22:15–22). Jesus points out that people who carry and use Caesar's coins should pay Caesar what belongs to him—while not forgetting to recognize the supreme claim of God. When the Sadducees try to show that belief in the resurrection of the dead is laughable and contrary to the Pentateuch, Jesus replies that they understand neither the life-giving power of the Creator God nor the lasting bond he creates with the patriarchs in the Pentateuch. To the Pharisee's question about the greatest commandment, Jesus replies that the heart of the law is love of God and neighbor; the rest of the law is to be interpreted and judged by the standard of love (22:34–40). Jesus then goes on the attack with his question about the son of David who is David's Lord (22:41–46). His question reduces these teachers to silence. He alone is the legitimate teacher.

Jesus Warns Against the Teachers of the Law and the Pharisees
(Also Mark 12.38–39; Luke 11.43,46; 20.45–46)

23 Then Jesus spoke to the crowds and to his disciples. [2]"The teachers of the Law and the Pharisees," he said, "are the authorized interpreters of Moses' Law. [3]So you must obey and follow everything they tell you to do;

do not, however, imitate their actions, because they do not practice what they preach. ⁴They fix up heavy loads and tie them on men's backs, yet they aren't willing even to lift a finger to help them carry those loads. ⁵They do everything just so people will see them. See how big are the containers with scripture verses on their foreheads and arms, and notice how long are the hems of their cloaks! ⁶They love the best places at feasts and the reserved seats in the synagogues; ⁷they love to be greeted with respect in the marketplaces and have people call them 'Teacher.' ⁸You must not be called 'Teacher,' for you are all brothers of one another and have only one Teacher. ⁹And you must not call anyone here on earth 'Father,' for you have only the one Father in heaven. ¹⁰Nor should you be called 'Leader,' because your one and only leader is the Messiah. ¹¹The greatest one among you must be your servant. ¹²And whoever makes himself great will be humbled, and whoever humbles himself will be made great.''

Jesus Condemns Their Hypocrisy
(Also Mark 12.40; Luke 11.39–42,44,52; 20.47)

¹³"How terrible for you, teachers of the Law and Pharisees! Impostors! You lock the door to the Kingdom of heaven in men's faces, but you yourselves will not go in, and neither will you let people in who are trying to go in!

[¹⁴"How terrible for you, teachers of the Law and Pharisees! Impostors! You take advantage of widows and rob them of their homes, and then make a show of saying long prayers! Because of this your punishment will be all the worse!]

¹⁵"How terrible for you, teachers of the Law and Pharisees! Impostors! You sail the seas and cross whole countries to win one convert; and when you succeed, you make him twice as deserving of going to hell as you yourselves are!

¹⁶"How terrible for you, blind guides! You teach, 'If a man swears by the Temple he isn't bound by his vow; but if he swears by the gold in the Temple, he is bound.' ¹⁷Blind fools! Which is more important, the gold or the Temple which makes the gold holy? ¹⁸You also teach, 'If a man swears by the altar he isn't bound by his vow; but if he swears by the gift on the altar, he is bound.' ¹⁹How blind you are! Which is more important, the gift or the altar which makes the gift holy? ²⁰So then, when a man swears by the altar he is swearing by it and by all the gifts on it; ²¹and when a man swears by the Temple he is swearing by it and by God, the one who lives there; ²²and when a man swears by heaven he is swearing by God's throne and by him who sits on it.

²³"How terrible for you, teachers of the Law and Pharisees! Impostors! You give to God one tenth even of the seasoning herbs, such as mint, dill, and cumin, but you neglect to obey the really important teachings of the Law, such as justice and mercy and honesty. These you should practice, without neglecting the others. ²⁴Blind guides! You strain a fly out of your drink, but swallow a camel.

²⁵"How terrible for you, teachers of the Law and Pharisees! Impostors! You clean the outside of your cup and plate, while the inside is full of things you have gotten by violence and selfishness. ²⁶Blind Pharisee! Clean what is inside the cup first, and then the outside will be clean too!

²⁷"How terrible for you, teachers of the Law and Pharisees! Impostors! You are like white-washed tombs, which look fine on the outside, but are full of dead men's bones and rotten stuff on the inside. ²⁸In the same way, on the outside you appear to everybody as good, but inside you are full of lies and sins."

Jesus Predicts Their Punishment
(Also Luke 11.47–51)

²⁹"How terrible for you, teachers of the Law and Pharisees! Impostors! You make fine tombs for the prophets, and decorate the monuments of those who lived good lives, ³⁰and you say, 'If we had lived long ago in the time of our ancestors, we would not have done what they did and killed the prophets.' ³¹So you actually admit that you are the descendants of those who murdered the prophets! ³²Go on, then, and finish up what your ancestors started! ³³Snakes, and sons of snakes! How do you expect to escape from being condemned to hell? ³⁴And so I tell you: I will send you prophets and wise men and teachers; you will kill some of them, nail others to the cross, and whip others in your synagogues, and chase them from town to town. ³⁵As a result, the punishment for the murder of all innocent men will fall on you, from the murder of innocent Abel to the murder of Zechariah, Berechiah's son, whom you murdered between the Temple and the altar. ³⁶I tell you indeed: the punishment for all these will fall upon the people of this day!"

³⁷"O Jerusalem, Jerusalem! You kill the prophets and stone the messengers God has sent you! How many times have I wanted to put my arms around all your people, just as a

hen gathers her chicks under her wings, but you would not let me! [38]Now your home will be completely forsaken. [39]From now on you will never see me again, I tell you, until you say, 'God bless him who comes in the name of the Lord.' "

Hypocrisy

Having vanquished his foes in these disputes, Jesus now pronounces judgment upon them in chapter 23. Jesus first warns the crowds and his disciples to avoid the hypocrisy of the scribes and Pharisees as well as their love of deference and titles (23:1–12). Then follow the seven woes upon the hypocritical scribes and Pharisees (23:13–36). Jesus severely denounces the Jewish teachers for hindering entrance into the kingdom, for pursuing foreign missions which only make converts worse than their teachers, for their casuistry concerning oaths, for their neglect of great obligations while they are absorbed with small points, for their concern about exterior cleanliness rather than interior morality, for their external propriety which hides internal corruption, and finally for being of one mind with their forefathers who murdered the prophets in the past, with the hint that they, the current citizens of Jerusalem will do the same to him (23:37–39). The result of this final rejection of God's messengers will be the final rejection of Jerusalem.

Jesus Speaks of the Destruction of the Temple
(Also Mark 13.1–2; Luke 21.5–6)

24 Jesus left and was going away from the Temple when his disciples came to him to show him the Temple's buildings. [2]"Yes," he said, "you may well look at all these. I tell you this: not a single stone here will be left in its place; every one of them will be thrown down."

Troubles and Persecutions
(Also Mark 13.3—13; Luke 21.7—19)

[3]As Jesus sat on the Mount of Olives, the disciples came to him in private. "Tell us when all this will be" they asked, "and what will happen to show that it is the time for your coming and the end of the age."

[4]Jesus answered: "Watch out, and do not let anyone fool you. [5]Because many men will come in my name, saying, 'I am the Messiah!' and fool many people. [6]You are going to hear the noise of battles closeby and the news of battles far away; but, listen, do not be troubled. Such things must happen, but they do not mean that the end has come. [7]One country will fight another country, one kingdom will attack another kingdom. There will be famines and earthquakes everywhere. [8]All these things are like the first pains of childbirth.

[9]"Then men will arrest you and hand you over to be punished, and you will be put to death. All mankind will hate you because of me. [10]Many will give up their faith at that time; they will betray each other and hate each other. [11]Then many false prophets will appear and fool many people. [12]Such will be the spread of evil that many people's love will grow cold. [13]But the person who holds out to the end will be saved. [14]And this Good News about the Kingdom will be preached through all the world, for a witness to all mankind—and then will come the end."

The Awful Horror
(Also Mark 13.14—23; Luke 21.20—24)

[15]"You will see 'The Awful Horror,' of which the prophet Daniel spoke, standing in the holy place." (Note to the reader: understand what this means!) [16]"Then those who are in Judea must run away to the hills. [17]The man who is on the roof of his house must not take the time to go down and get his belongings from the house. [18]The man who is in the field must not go back to get his cloak. [19]How terrible it will be in those days for women who are pregnant, and for mothers who have little babies! [20]Pray to God that you will not have to run away during the winter or on a Sabbath! [21]For the trouble at that time will be far more terrible than any there has ever been, from the beginning of the world to this very day. Nor will there ever be anything like it. [22]But God has already reduced the number of days; had he not done so, nobody would survive. For the sake of his chosen people, however, God will reduce the days.

[23]"Then, if anyone says to you, 'Look, here is the Messiah!' or 'There he is!'—do not believe him. [24]For false Messiahs and false prophets will appear; they will perform great signs and wonders for the purpose of deceiving God's chosen people, if possible. [25]Listen! I have told you this ahead of time.

[26]"Or, if people should tell you, 'Look, he is out in the desert!'—don't go there; or if they say, 'Look, he is hiding here!'—don't believe it. [27]For the Son of Man will come like the lightning which flashes across the whole sky from the east to the west.

[28]"Wherever there is a dead body the vultures will gather."

The Coming of the Son of Man
(Also Mark 13.24–27; Luke 21.25–28)

[29]"Soon after the trouble of those days the sun will grow dark, the moon will no longer shine, the stars will fall from heaven, and the powers in space will be driven from their course. [30]Then the sign of the Son of Man will appear in the sky; then all the tribes of earth will weep, and they will see the Son of Man coming on the clouds of heaven with power and great glory. [31]The great trumpet will sound, and he will send out his angels to the four corners of the earth, and they will gather his chosen people from one end of the world to the other."

The Lesson of the Fig Tree
(Also Mark 13.28–31; Luke 21.29–33)

[32]"Let the fig tree teach you a lesson. When its branches become green and tender, and it starts putting out leaves, you know that summer is near. [33]In the same way, when you see all these things, you will know that the time is near, ready to begin. [34]Remember this! All these things will happen before the people now living have all died. [35]Heaven and earth will pass away; my words will never pass away."

[36]"No one knows, however, when that day and hour will come—neither the angels in heaven, nor the Son; the Father alone knows.

After speaking judgment on the Jewish leaders, Jesus speaks of the final judgment of the whole world in the fifth and final discourse, the eschatological or apocalyptic discourse (chapters 24 and 25). There are two main parts of the eschatological discourse. The first part, 24:1–36, is taken over from Mark. More doctrinal in tone, it treats of the chain of events which will lead to the parousia (that is, the second coming of Christ). Jesus symbolically leaves the Temple (as Matthew's Church has left the synagogue) and prophesies the Temple's destruction (24:1–2). In what follows, Matthew, writing between A.D. 80 and 90, carefully distinguishes the destruction of the Temple (A.D. 70) from the end of the world. Jesus warns against being shaken by various political, natural, and religious convulsions. These constitute not the end of the world, but only the beginning of the painful period before his return (24:3–8). Upset in the world will be paralleled by upset in the Church, brought about by both persecution from without and immorality within (24:9–14). In these verses, Matthew reflects the tension wracking his own Church. He bids the faithful members to hold fast to the Gospel of love. Matthew then turns to the Jewish War (A.D. 66–70) which ended with the destruction of Jerusalem (24:15–22). This disaster, already lying in the past for Matthew's Church, acts as a foreshadowing and a warning of the still greater cataclysm to come. The situation of the Church after the Jewish War is depicted in 24:23–28: it is one of bewilderment which arises out of the claims of false prophets. The claim of these religious leaders that their truth is for the chosen few reveals them to be false, for Christ's coming will be public and glorious. Only after the Church has endured all these afflictions will this world pass away completely as Jesus the Son of Man comes to judge the wicked and save his chosen ones (24:29–31). The Markan part of the discourse ends with the parable of the fig tree (24:32–36), stressing that the end will certainly come soon. Yet it is not open to calculation.

[37]"The coming of the Son of Man will be like what happened in the time of Noah. [38]Just as in the days before the Flood, people ate and drank, men and women married, up to the very day Noah went into the ark; [39]yet they did not know what was happening until the Flood came and swept them all away. That is how it will be when the Son of Man comes. [40]At that time two men will be working in the field: one will be taken away, the other will be left behind. [41]Two women will be at the mill grinding meal: one will be taken away, the other will be left behind. [42]Watch out, then, because you do not know what day your Lord will come. [43]Remember this: if the man of the house knew the time when the thief would come, he would stay awake and not let the thief break into his house. [44]For this reason, then, you also must be always ready, because the Son of Man will come at an hour when you are not expecting him."

The Faithful or the Unfaithful Servant
(Also Luke 12.41–48)

[45]"Who, then, is the faithful and wise servant? He is the one whom his master has placed in charge of the other servants, to give them their food at the proper time. [46]How happy is that servant if his master finds him doing this when he comes home! [47]Indeed, I tell you, the master will put that servant in charge of all his property. [48]But if he is a bad servant, he will tell himself, 'My master will not come back for a long time,' [49]and he will begin to beat his fellow servants, and eat and drink with drunkards. [50]Then that servant's master will come back some day when he does not expect him and at a time he does not know; [51]the master

will cut him to pieces, and make him share the fate of the impostors. There he will cry and gnash his teeth.''

The Parable of the Ten Girls

25 "On that day the Kingdom of heaven will be like ten girls who took their oil lamps and went out to meet the bridegroom. [2]Five of them were foolish, and the other five were wise. [3]The foolish ones took their lamps but did not take any extra oil with them, [4]while the wise ones took containers full of oil with their lamps. [5]The bridegroom was late in coming, so the girls began to nod and fall asleep.

[6]"It was already midnight when the cry rang out, 'Here is the bridegroom! Come and meet him!' [7]The ten girls woke up and trimmed their lamps. [8]Then the foolish ones said to the wise ones, 'Let us have some of your oil, because our lamps are going out.' [9]'No, indeed,' the wise ones answered back, 'there is not enough for you and us. Go to the store and buy some for yourselves.' [10]So the foolish girls went off to buy some oil, and while they were gone the bridegroom arrived. The five girls who were ready went in with him to the wedding feast, and the door was closed.

[11]"Later the other girls arrived. 'Sir, sir! Let us in!' they cried. [12]'But I really don't know you,' the bridegroom answered.'' [13]And Jesus concluded, "Watch out, then, because you do not know the day or hour.''

[14]"It will be like a man who was about to leave home on a trip: he called his servants and put them in charge of his property. [15]He gave to each one according to his ability: to one he

gave five thousand dollars, to the other two thousand dollars, and to the other one thousand dollars. Then he left on his trip. [16]The servant who had received five thousand dollars went at once and invested his money and earned another five thousand dollars. [17]In the same way the servant who received two thousand dollars earned another two thousand dollars. [18]But the servant who received one thousand dollars went off, dug a hole in the ground, and hid his master's money.

[19]"After a long time the master of those servants came back and settled accounts with them. [20]The servant who had received five thousand dollars came in and handed over the other five thousand dollars. 'You gave me five thousand dollars, sir,' he said. 'Look! Here are another five thousand dollars that I have earned.' [21]"Well done, good and faithful servant!' said his master. 'You have been faithful in managing small amounts, so I will put you in charge of large amounts. Come on in, and share my happiness!' [22]Then the servant who had been given two thousand dollars came in and said, 'You gave me two thousand dollars, sir. Look! Here are another two thousand dollars that I have earned.' [23]"Well done, good and faithful servant!' said his master. 'You have been faithful in managing small amounts, so I will put you in charge of large amounts. Come on in and share my happiness!' [24]Then the servant who had received one thousand dollars came in and said: 'Sir, I know you are a hard man: you reap harvests where you did not plant, and gather crops where you did not scatter seed. [25]I was afraid, so I went off and hid your money in the ground. Look! Here is what belongs to you.' [26]"You bad and lazy servant!' his master said. 'You knew, did you, that I reap

harvests where I did not plant, and gather crops where I did not scatter seed? [27]Well, then, you should have deposited my money in the bank, and I would have received it all back with interest when I returned. [28]Now, take the money away from him and give it to the one who has ten thousand dollars. [29]For to every one who has, even more will be given, and he will have more than enough; but the one who has nothing, even the little he has will be taken away from him. [30]As for this useless servant—throw him outside in the darkness; there he will cry and gnash his teeth.' "

The Final Judgment

[31]"When the Son of Man comes as King, and all the angels with him, he will sit on his royal throne, [32]and all the earth's people will be gathered before him. Then he will divide them into two groups, just as a shepherd separates the sheep from the goats. [33]He will put the sheep at his right and the goats at his left. [34]Then the King will say to the people on his right, 'You who are blessed by my Father! Come and receive the kingdom which has been prepared for you ever since the creation of the world. [35]I was hungry and you fed me, thirsty and you gave me drink; I was a stranger and you received me in your homes, [36]naked and you clothed me; I was sick and you took care of me, in prison and you visited me.' [37]The righteous will then answer him, 'When Lord, did we ever see you hungry and feed you, or thirsty and give you drink? [38]When did we ever see you a stranger and welcome you in our homes, or naked and clothe you? [39]When did we ever see you sick or in prison, and visit you? [40]The King will answer back, 'I tell you, indeed, whenever you did this

for one of the least important of these brothers of mine, you did it for me!'

⁴¹"Then he will say to those on his left, 'Away from me, you who are under God's curse! Away to the eternal fire which has been prepared for the Devil and his angels! ⁴²I was hungry but you would not feed me, thirsty but you would not give me drink; ⁴³ I was a stranger but you would not welcome me in your homes, naked but you would not clothe me; I was sick and in prison but you would not take care of me.' ⁴⁴Then they will answer him, 'When, Lord, did we ever see you hungry, or thirsty, or a stranger, or naked, or sick, or in prison, and we would not help you?' ⁴⁵The King will answer them back, 'I tell you, indeed, whenever you refused to help one of these least important ones, you refused to help me.' ⁴⁶These, then, will be sent off to eternal punishment; the righteous will go to eternal life."

The Plot Against Jesus
(Also Mark 14.1–2; Luke 22.1–2; John 11.45–53)

26 When Jesus had finished teaching all these things, he said to his disciples, ²"In two days, as you know, it will be the Feast of Passover, and the Son of Man will be handed over to be nailed to the cross."

Watch and Pray

The second half of the discourse, which, with few exceptions, has no parallel in Mark, is more exhortatory in tone (24:37—25:46). Up to now Matthew has been throwing cold water on fiery apocalyptic dreams. In what follows he will try to awaken a healthy eschatological tension in Christians who are being put to sleep by the droning of this world. The tone of vigilance is set in 24:37–44 by short introductory parables (Noah, the people in the field and at the mill, the householder and the thief). The necessity of vigilance during the "delay" of the Lord's return is then hammered home at great length by the parables of the responsible or irresponsible servant (24:45–51), the prudent and foolish virgins (25:1–13), and the three servants entrusted with large sums of money (25:14–30). In each of these parables, Matthew inserts a reference to the long time which elapses before the master or bridegroom arrives on the scene. The entire discourse ends with the grand scene of the last judgment (25:31–46). The standard by which people will be judged is the standard of love, translated into concrete acts of mercy. And that standard in turn is revealed to be a Christological standard; the act of mercy extended to the suffering is extended to the Son of Man, who identifies himself with the poor and outcast of humankind. This identification will now be acted out as the Son of Man, who is judge, becomes the suffering and risen Son of Man in chapters 26–28.

The whole of the Gospel, with all its lengthy discourses, aims at the good news of the death and resurrection of Jesus. For Matthew the death-resurrection of Jesus becomes one apocalyptic event which shakes the foundations of the old world and ushers in the kingdom. The death-resurrection is the great turning point of salvation history, and, accordingly, Matthew unites the two events.

As we read these chapters we must keep our eyes focused first of all on Jesus. We should notice how Matthew constantly heightens the dignity and majesty of Jesus, even in his suffering and death. The other persons around Jesus—Peter, Judas, the woman who anoints him, the women at the cross and grave, Pilate and his wife, the chief priests, the soldiers—all reflect positive or negative attitudes toward the crucified and risen Jesus, and so provide exhortation or warning to the members of Matthew's Church. Throughout the passion, Matthew's only continuous source is Mark. It is important, therefore, to keep a copy of Mark 14—15 close at hand, to see how Matthew reinterprets Mark, and so brings to expression a new theological vision.

Matthew begins this section by noting that Jesus has finished his five great discourses: "has finished teaching *all* these things." Where Mark simply mentions the time when the plot was hatched against Jesus, Matthew has a fourth prediction of the passion.

■ *Reflection*

According to the standards set by the Gospel, how would I be judged, were I part of Matthew's judgment scene?

---

³Then the chief priests and the Jewish elders met together in the palace of Caiaphas, the High Priest, ⁴and made plans to arrest Jesus secretly and put him to death. ⁵"We must not do it during the feast," they said, "or the people will riot."

⁶While Jesus was at the house of Simon the leper, in Bethany, ⁷a woman came to him with an alabaster jar filled with an expensive perfume, which she poured on Jesus' head as he was eating. ⁸The disciples saw this and became angry. "Why all this waste?" they asked. ⁹"This perfume could have been sold for a large amount and the money given to the poor!" ¹⁰Jesus was aware of what they were saying and said to them: "Why are you bothering this woman? It is a fine and beautiful thing that she has done for me. ¹¹You will always have poor people with you, but I will not be with you al-

ways. ¹²What she did was to pour this perfume on my body to get me ready for burial. ¹³Now, remember this! Wherever this gospel is preached, all over the world, what she has done will be told in memory of her.''

¹⁴Then one of the twelve disciples—the one named Judas Iscariot—went to the chief priests ¹⁵and said, ''What will you give me if I hand Jesus over to you?'' So they counted out thirty silver coins and gave them to him. ¹⁶From then on Judas was looking for a good chance to betray Jesus.

The Conspiracy

Note the ''then'' at the beginning of 26:3. It implies that the events of the passion narrative took place only after Jesus had predicted the time and circumstance. The scene is reminiscent of the first plot against Jesus' life, when the chief priests and scribes gathered with Herod to plan the death of the predicted king at the time of Jesus' birth.

The plotters specify that the arrest and murder of Jesus are not to take place during the feast. Yet they do. This is most likely a sign that Jesus' desire to link his death and resurrection with the Passover cannot be negated by the political concern of his enemies.

Anointing one's head at a festive banquet was customary (see Psalm 23:5). In this case, however, the disciples complain about the extravagance. Jesus defends the woman against the short-sighted objections of the disciples on two grounds. He is about to die. This is the only reference in Matthew to the anointing for burial. Secondly, Jesus points out that the poor will always be present to receive alms, but he would soon be unable to receive such an honor.

Jesus' lack of concern for money is contrasted with Judas' accepting payment for his act of betrayal. The thirty pieces of silver reflect two Old Testament texts: Zechariah 11:12 and Exodus 21:32. The sum is a small amount, a demeaning price for so great a life.

Jesus Eats the Passover Meal with His Disciples
(Also Mark 14.12–21; Luke 22.7–14, 21–23; John 13.21–30)

[17]On the first day of the Feast of Unleavened Bread the disciples came to Jesus and asked him, "Where do you want us to get the Passover supper ready for you?" [18]"Go to a certain man in the city," he said to them, "and tell him: 'The Teacher says, My hour has come; my disciples and I will celebrate the Passover at your house.' " [19]The disciples did as Jesus had told them and prepared the Passover supper.

[20]When it was evening Jesus and the twelve disciples sat down to eat. [21]During the meal Jesus said, "I tell you, one of you will betray me." [22]The disciples were very upset and began to ask him, one after the other, "Surely you don't mean me, Lord?" [23]Jesus answered: "One who dips his bread in the dish with me will betray me. [24]The Son of Man will die as the Scriptures say he will, but how terrible for that man who will betray the Son of Man! It would have been better for that man if he had never been born!" [25]Judas, the traitor, spoke up. "Surely you don't mean me, Teacher?" he asked. Jesus answered, "So you say."

[26]While they were eating, Jesus took the bread, gave a prayer of thanks, broke it, and gave it to his disciples. "Take and eat it." he said; "this is my body." [27]Then he took the cup,

gave thanks to God, and gave it to them. "Drink it, all of you," he said; [28]"for this is my blood, which seals God's covenant, my blood poured out for many for the forgiveness of sins. [29]I tell you, I will never again drink this wine until the day I drink the new wine with you in my Father's Kingdom." [30]Then they sang a hymn and went out to the Mount of Olives.

[31]Then Jesus said to them: "This very night all of you will run away and leave me, for the scripture says, 'God will kill the shepherd and the sheep of the flock will be scattered.' [32]But after I am raised to life I will go to Galilee ahead of you." [33]Peter spoke up and said to Jesus, "I will never leave you, even though all the rest do!" [34]"Remember this!" Jesus said to Peter. "Before the rooster crows tonight you will say three times that you do not know me." [35]Peter answered, "I will never say I do not know you, even if I have to die with you!" And all the disciples said the same thing.

Holy Thursday

In the account of the preparation for the Passover meal, Matthew indicates that Jesus is in control. He directs the disciples to speak to the host, and to tell him that his "hour has come." So great is the feeling of Jesus' mastery of the events that the disciples see his words about his betrayer not as a prediction, but as a statement. They wonder which one will be cast in this role. Judas, however, has already taken on the task. Like all other unbelievers in Matthew, he addresses Jesus as "Master." The other disciples call Jesus "Lord." To appreciate the richness of Matthew's version of the institution of the Eucharist, you might want to have before you all four versions of the institution found in the New Testament: the basically Markan form, found in

Mark 14:22–25 and Matthew 26:26–29, and the basically Pauline form in 1 Corinthians 11:23–25 and Luke 22:19–20. The important point is that each form is intended to be different, so one should not read one version into another.

In Matthew, the words over the cup are especially rich theologically. "My blood which seals God's covenant" refers directly to the sacrifice in Exodus 24:8. The blood of Jesus is said to be poured out "for many." This does not indicate that Jesus meant to limit the number of those included in the new covenant, simply that the sacrifice was not for himself alone. Matthew also adds to Mark's words over the cup: "for the forgiveness of sins," referring back to the words of the angel in the infancy narrative (1:21).

Jesus' reference to drinking the "new wine" with the disciples in the kingdom signals that their fellowship will be broken by his death, but taken up again after the resurrection. This theme is echoed in his remarks on the Mount of Olives. Now they will be "scattered" but soon reunited in Galilee.

■ *Reflection*
How is my appreciation of the Eucharist deepened by my understanding of the Gospel?

Jesus Prays in Gethsemane
(Also Mark 14.32–42; Luke 22.39–46)

[36]Then Jesus went with his disciples to a place called Gethsemane, and he said to them, "Sit here while I go over there and pray." [37]He took with him Peter, and Zebedee's two sons. Grief and anguish came over him, [38]and he said to them, "The sorrow in my heart is so great that it almost crushes me. Stay here and watch

with me" ³⁹He went a little farther on, threw himself face down to the ground, and prayed, "My Father, if it is possible, take this cup away from me! But not what I want, but what you want."

⁴⁰Then he returned to the three disciples and found them asleep; and he said to Peter: "How is it that you three were not able to watch with me for one hour? ⁴¹Keep watch, and pray, so you will not fall into temptation. The spirit is willing, but the flesh is weak."

⁴²Again a second time Jesus went away and prayed, "My Father, if this cup cannot be taken away unless I drink it, your will be done." ⁴³He returned once more and found the disciples asleep; they could not keep their eyes open.

⁴⁴Again Jesus left them, went away, and prayed the third time, saying the same words. ⁴⁵Then he returned to the disciples and said: "Are you still sleeping and resting? Look! The hour has come for the Son of Man to be handed over to the power of sinful men. ⁴⁶Rise, let us go. Look, here is the man who is betraying me!"

One of the great themes of Jesus' prayer in Gethsemane (26:36–46) is his fellowship with the disciples. The cup was an Old Testament symbol of one's fate. At the Last Supper, the disciples had joined in the sharing of the cup; they accepted a share in Jesus' fate. Now they are asleep—unwilling, or unable, at this "hour" to fulfill their commitment. Another level of meaning here is for the members of Matthew's Church. They who have accepted the eucharistic cup must be prepared to accept the responsibilities of discipleship.

The Arrest of Jesus
(Also Mark 14.43–50; Luke 22.47–53; John 18.3–12)

⁴⁷He was still talking when Judas, one of the twelve disciples, arrived. With him was a large crowd carrying swords and clubs, sent by the chief priests and the Jewish elders. ⁴⁸The traitor had given the crowd a signal: "The man I kiss is the one you want. Arrest him!" ⁴⁹When Judas arrived he went straight to Jesus and said, "Peace be with you, Teacher," and kissed him. ⁵⁰Jesus answered, "Be quick about it, friend!" Then they came up, arrested Jesus and held him tight. ⁵¹One of those who were with Jesus drew his sword and struck at the High Priest's slave, cutting off his ear. ⁵²Then Jesus said to him: "Put your sword back in its place, for all who take the sword will die by the sword. ⁵³Don't you know that I could call on my Father for help and at once he would send me more than twelve armies of angels? ⁵⁴But in that case, how could the Scriptures come true that say it must happen in this way?"

⁵⁵Then Jesus spoke to the crowd: "Did you have to come with swords and clubs to capture me, as though I were an outlaw? Every day I sat down and taught in the Temple, and you did not arrest me. ⁵⁶But all this has happened to make come true what the prophets wrote in the Scriptures." Then all the disciples left him and ran away.

⁵⁷Those who had arrested Jesus took him to the house of Caiaphas, the High Priest, where the teachers of the Law and the elders had gathered together. ⁵⁸Peter followed him from a distance, as far as the courtyard of the High Priest's house. He went into the courtyard and sat down with the guards, to see how it would all come out. ⁵⁹The chief priests and the whole

Council tried to find some false evidence against Jesus, to put him to death; [60]but they could not find any, even though many came up and told lies about him. Finally two men stepped forward [61]and said, "This man said, 'I am able to tear down God's Temple and three days later build it back up.' "

[62]The High Priest stood up and said to Jesus, "Have you no answer to give to this accusation against you?" [63]But Jesus kept quiet. Again the High Priest spoke to him: "In the name of the living God, I now put you on oath: tell us if you are the Messiah, the Son of God." [64]Jesus answered him: "So you say. But I tell all of you: from this time on you will see the Son of Man sitting at the right side of the Almighty, and coming on the clouds of heaven!" [65]At this the High Priest tore his clothes and said: "Blasphemy! We don't need any more witnesses! Right here you have heard his wicked words! [66]What do you think?" They answered, "He is guilty, and must die."

[67]Then they spat in his face and beat him; and those who slapped him [68]said, "Prophesy for us, Messiah! Tell us who hit you!"

[69]Peter was sitting outside in the courtyard, when one of the High Priest's servant girls came to him and said, "You, too, were with Jesus of Galilee." [70]But he denied it in front of them all. "I don't know what you are talking about," he answered, [71]and went on out to the entrance of the courtyard. Another servant girl saw him and said to the men there, "He was with Jesus of Nazareth." [72]Again Peter denied it, and answered. "I swear that I don't know that man!" [73]After a little while the men standing there came to Peter. "Of course you are one of them," they said. "After all, the way you

speak gives you away!" 74Then Peter made a vow: "May God punish me if I am not telling the truth! I do not know that man!" Just then a rooster crowed, 75and Peter remembered what Jesus had told him, "Before the rooster crows, you will say three times that you do not know me." He went out and wept bitterly.

Arrest and Trials

In the narrative of Jesus' arrest (26:47–56), Jesus' statement to Judas in verse 50 once again brings out Matthew's theme of Jesus being in control of the events. It is Jesus who directs the outcome, even to the point of forbidding his own defense. Matthew uses the incident of the cutting of the slave's ear to insert Jesus' order to put up the sword. He gives three reasons for his order. The most important of the three is that Jesus is allowing all this to happen so that "the Scriptures (can) come true."

In narrating the story of the trial, Matthew emphasizes that the Sanhedrin (the supreme court for Jews in religious and legal matters) seeks *false* witnesses from the very start. Yet when it comes to the famous saying about destroying the Temple, Matthew does not explicitly say that the two witnesses were false, for Jesus does say, "I can destroy. . . ." The truth of the statement is borne out in future events. The power of the Temple is destroyed at Jesus' death and at the final destruction of Jerusalem in A.D. 70. It is realized again in a new way in the resurrected Jesus and in the Church.

The silence of Jesus before his judges recalls the suffering servant of Isaiah 53:7. Mark has Jesus answer "I am" to the question of the high priest. Jesus in Matthew repeats what he said to Judas in 26:25. Jesus then adds the truth which is lacking in the high priest's conception of Christ and Son of God: the Messiah is also the Son of Man.

In contrast to Jesus' acknowledgment of the truth about himself, the story of the denial brings out how Peter not only claims not to know Jesus, but also denies the relationship between them. As a continuing sign of God's mercy for repentant sinners, Peter immediately regrets his behavior. His reaction is sorrow.

Judas' reaction to the realization of his sin, however, is despair. His remorse is not repentance. But even in his death he is the agent of fulfillment of Old Testament prophecy. His action also introduces the theme in chapter 27 of Jesus' innocence.

Jesus Is Taken to Pilate
(Also Mark 15.1; Luke 23.1–2; John 18.28–32)

27 Early in the morning all the chief priests and the Jewish elders made their plan against Jesus to put him to death. ²They put him in chains, took him, and handed him over to Pilate, the Governor.

³When Judas, the traitor, saw that Jesus had been condemned, he repented and took back the thirty silver coins to the chief priests and the elders. ⁴"I have sinned by betraying an innocent man to death!" he said, "What do we care about that?" they answered. "That is your business!" ⁵Judas threw the money into the sanctuary and left them; then he went off and hanged himself.

⁶The chief priests picked up the money and said, "This is blood money, and it is against our Law to put it in the Temple treasury." ⁷After reaching an agreement about it, they used

the money to buy Potter's Field, as a cemetery for foreigners. ⁸That is why that field is called "Field of Blood" to this very day.

⁹Then what the prophet Jeremiah had said came true: "They took the thirty silver coins (the amount the people of Israel had agreed to pay for him), ¹⁰and used them to buy the potter's field, as the Lord commanded me."

¹¹Jesus stood before the Governor, who questioned him. "Are you the king of the Jews?" he asked. "So you say," answered Jesus. ¹²He said nothing, however, to the accusations of the chief priests and elders. ¹³So Pilate said to him, "Don't you hear all these things they accuse you of?" ¹⁴But Jesus refused to answer a single word, so that the Governor was greatly surprised.

¹⁵At every Passover Feast the Governor was in the habit of setting free any prisoner the crowd asked for. ¹⁶At that time there was a well-known prisoner named Jesus Barabbas. ¹⁷So when the crowd gathered, Pilate asked them, "Which one do you want me to set free for you, Jesus Barabbas or Jesus called the Christ?" ¹⁸He knew very well that they had handed Jesus over to him because they were jealous.

¹⁹While Pilate was sitting in the judgment hall, his wife sent him a message: "Have nothing to do with that innocent man, because in a dream last night I suffered much on account of him."

²⁰The chief priests and the elders persuaded the crowds to ask Pilate to set Barabbas free and have Jesus put to death. ²¹But the Governor asked them, "Which one of these two do you want me to set free for you?" "Barabbas!" they answered. ²²"What, then, shall I do with

Jesus called the Christ?" Pilate asked them. "Nail him to the cross!" they all answered. ²³But Pilate asked, "What crime has he committed?" Then they started shouting at the top of their voices, "Nail him to the cross!" ²⁴When Pilate saw it was no use to go on, but that a riot might break out, he took some water, washed his hands in front of the crowd, and said, "I am not responsible for the death of this man! This is your doing!" ²⁵The whole crowd answered back, "Let the punishment for his death fall on us and on our children!" ²⁶Then Pilate set Barabbas free for them; he had Jesus whipped and handed him over to be nailed to the cross.

²⁷Then Pilate's soldiers took Jesus into the Governor's palace, and the whole company gathered around him. ²⁸They stripped off his clothes and put a scarlet robe on him. ²⁹Then they made a crown out of thorny branches and put it on his head, and put a stick in his right hand; then they knelt before him and made fun of him. "Long live the King of the Jews!" they said. ³⁰They spat on him, and took the stick and hit him over the head. ³¹When they finished making fun of him, they took the robe off and put his own clothes back on him, and then led him out to nail him to the cross.

Good Friday

The story of Jesus before Pilate points up this innocence in contrast to the guilt of Pilate, Barabbas, and the crowd. Israel stands at the crossroads of its history. Will they choose the Messiah who will bring back to Israel the reign of God, or the Zealot with his promises of an earthly kingdom? Matthew clearly makes the choice universal: " 'Crucify him!' they *all* answered," and "The *whole crowd* answered, 'Let the responsibility of his death . . .'."

Writing after A.D. 70 Matthew may see the destruction of Jerusalem as a sign of the end of Israel brought about by this one fateful decision. Events will now show that Israel has given up the right to be God's people. The Church now fills that role. The unique events narrated by Matthew, the dream of Pilate's wife and the washing of hands heighten the sense of Jesus' innocence, thus emphasizing even more the guilt of those who would put him to death.

Notice, by the way, how the scourging, the crowning with thorns, and the actual event of nailing Jesus to the cross are all narrated quickly and soberly. The brutal and bloody aspects of these events are not dwelt upon for their own sake. The emphasis seen in the scene of mockery (27:27–31) is on the words of the soldiers, who unwittingly proclaim the truth.

Jesus Is Crucified
(Also Mark 15.21–32; Luke 23.26–43; John 19.17–27)

³²As they were going out they met a man from Cyrene named Simon, and they forced him to carry Jesus' cross. ³³They came to a place called Golgotha, which means "The Place of the Skull." ³⁴There they offered him wine to drink, mixed with gall; after tasting it, however, he would not drink it.

³⁵They nailed him to the cross, and then divided his clothes among them by throwing dice. ³⁶After that they sat there and watched him. ³⁷Above his head they put the written notice of the accusation against him: "This is Jesus, the King of the Jews." ³⁸Then they

nailed two bandits to crosses with Jesus, one on his right and the other on his left.

[39]People passing by shook their heads and threw insults at Jesus: [40]"You were going to tear down the Temple and build it up in three days! Save yourself, if you are God's Son! Come on down from the cross!" [41]In the same way the chief priests and the teachers of the Law and the elders made fun of him: [42]"He saved others but he cannot save himself! Isn't he the King of Israel? If he will come down off the cross now, we will believe in him! [43]He trusts in God and says he is God's Son. Well, then, let us see if God wants to save him now!" [44]Even the bandits who had been crucified with him insulted him in the same way.

[45]At noon the whole country was covered with darkness, which lasted for three hours. [46]At about three o'clock Jesus cried out with a loud shout, *Eli, Eli, lema sabachthani*? which means, "My God, my God, why did you abandon me?" [47]Some of the people standing there heard him and said, "He is calling for Elijah!" [48]One of them ran up at once, took a sponge, soaked it in wine, put it on the end of a stick, and tried to make him drink it. [49]But the others said, "Wait, let us see if Elijah is coming to save him!" [50]Jesus again gave a loud cry, and breathed his last.

[51]Then the curtain hanging in the Temple was torn in two, from top to bottom. The earth shook, the rocks split apart, [52]the graves broke open, and many of God's people who had died were raised to life. [53]They left the graves; and after Jesus rose from death they went into the Holy City, where many people saw them.

[54]When the army officer and the soldiers with him who were watching Jesus saw the

earthquake and everything else that happened, they were terrified and said, "He really was the Son of God!"

In the mention of Simon of Cyrene in 27:32, Matthew omits the family details mentioned in Mark 15:21, probably because Simon was not commonly known to members of his Church. Instead of the wine mixed with myrrh mentioned by Mark, Matthew carefully has the two drinks he mentions fulfill the prophecy of the suffering just man in Psalm 69:21. Notice how the two halves of the verse are fulfilled in Matthew 27:34 and 48. Although Matthew obviously sees a fulfillment of Psalm 22:18 in the dividing of Jesus' garments, he does not cite the verse explicitly.

In verse 43, Psalm 22 is used to describe the suffering of the just man. There also may be a reference of Wisdom 2:11–20, which adds the idea of Son of God to the theme of the suffering just man. The events of Jesus' death also reflect the events of the infancy narrative. Jesus is named savior and king by both Jews and gentiles. Unwittingly, his persecutors take the role of witnesses to the fulfillment of the prophecies concerning the Messiah.

As in the story of the temptation in the wilderness, Jesus refuses to react by using his divine power for human gratification. What is seen by his accusers as weakness is obvious strength to Matthew. The darkness over the whole earth (or land) expresses God's anger and judgment over the sin of man.

Trust in the Lord

Psalm 22 has been used at least three times by Matthew in the crucifixion scene. Now Jesus himself uses the initial words of the psalm to express his bitter suffering and sense of abandonment. But it is not a cry of despair. Pious Jews would immediately recognize Psalm 22 as the song of confidence in God amidst great suffering. Both the suffering and the trust are real, and to understand the significance of the event we cannot eliminate either.

In Matthew, 27:51–54 we have one of the most important statements of the Gospel on the meaning of Jesus' death. There are four basic apocalyptic events in this section, each in its own way proclaiming the breaking in of the new age at the death of Jesus. The fact that the curtain in the Temple is "torn in two" indicates the end of the importance of the Temple sacrifice as a means of communication with God. The earthquake describes the tumultuous breaking through of God's kingdom. This results in the evidence that Jesus' death brings life to others in the resurrection of the dead. Finally, the faith confession of the centurion is evidence of the mission that Jesus will give the disciples in 28:16–20, evidence also of the makeup of the community of the Church.

---

[55]There were many women there, looking on from a distance, who had followed Jesus from Galilee and helped him. [56]Among them were Mary Magdalene, Mary the mother of James and Joseph, and the mother of Zebedee's sons.

The Burial of Jesus
(Also Mark 15.42–47; Luke 23.50–56; John 19.38–42)

[57]When it was evening, a rich man from Arimathea arrived; his name was Joseph, and he also was a disciple of Jesus. [58]He went into the presence of Pilate and asked for the body of Jesus. Pilate gave orders for the body to be

given to Joseph. [59]So Joseph took it, wrapped it in a new linen sheet, [60]and placed it in his own grave, which he had just recently dug out of the rock, Then he rolled a large stone across the entrance to the grave and went away. [61]Mary Magdalene and the other Mary were sitting there, facing the grave.

[62]On the next day—that is, the day following Friday—the chief priests and the Pharisees met with Pilate [63]and said: "Sir, we remember that while that liar was still alive he said, 'I will be raised to life after three days.' [64]Give orders, then, for the grave to be safely guarded until the third day, so that his disciples will not be able to go and steal him, and then tell the people, 'He was raised from death.' This last lie would be even worse than the first one." [65]"Take a guard," Pilate told them; "go and guard the grave as best as you can." [66]So they left, and made the grave secure by putting a seal on the stone and leaving the guard on watch.

In 27:55–66 the events narrated seem to have as their main purpose several bits of evidence leading to the authenticity of the resurrection. The women are present at the crucifixion; they follow Jesus' body to the tomb, and, as is the Jewish custom of mourning, sit opposite the tomb once it is closed. The tomb is a new, or unused, one belonging to a wealthy person. There can be no mistaking its location, or the presence or absence of a single body. At the request of the Jewish leaders, a guard is set at the tomb, and a seal placed on the stone at the entrance. There can be little room for doubt that, on Sunday morning, the tomb would be found empty—the same tomb, by the same women—in spite of the guard and the seal.

That Jesus was raised from the dead can be argued by the Jews; that the tomb he was laid in was found empty cannot. This sets the stage for the narrative of the resurrection appearances.

■ *Reflection*

What relation has the account of Jesus' death with his discourses on true discipleship?

■ Discussion

1. What can we learn from Jesus' discourse in this section about the role the Church is to play in world events?

2. What insights into the meaning of the Eucharist can we gain from Matthew's account of the Last Supper?

3. What differences in character led Peter and Judas to two different responses in their denial of Jesus?

4. What can we learn about prayer from the events of the Last Supper, the garden at Gethsemane, and the crucifixion?

5. How do the renewed Holy Week liturgies better reflect the events of the passion, death, and resurrection as told in the Gospels?

■ Prayer and Meditation

"I will tell my people what you have done;
    I will praise you in their assembly:
'Praise him, you servants of the LORD!
    Honor him, you descendants of Jacob!
    Worship him, you people of Israel!
He does not neglect the poor or ignore their
      suffering;
    he does not turn away from them,
    but answers when they call for help.' "

Psalm 22:22–24

The Resurrection ———— Matthew 28

As we come to a discussion of the resurrection and the resurrection appearances in Matthew, it might be wise to preface our commentary with some general considerations about the resurrection.

No one saw the resurrection of Jesus. It is a mark of the sobriety of our canonical Gospels that, unlike later apocryphal gospels, they do not attempt to describe the resurrection or to claim that there were any witnesses to the actual event of Jesus' rising from the grave. Rather, the faith of the early Church derives mainly from the appearances of the risen Jesus to his disciples. The earliest testimony to the resurrection appearances is found in 1 Corinthians 15:3–7. We can see from the terse formula that the first Christians were interested in the fact of the appearances, which confirmed the truth of the resurrection. But neither Paul nor the pre-Pauline tradition ever gives us a detailed description of what a resurrection appearance looked like. Indeed, no precise time or place is mentioned. What is important is the "that," not the "how." The "that" of the resurrection and resurrection appearances is the bedrock of the earliest Christian preaching.

The "how" was left to be filled in by the later evangelists. Since there was no one normative description of the resurrection appearances, each evangelist was free, within the constraints of his particular tradition, to fill in the "how" according to his own theological insights. The resurrection appearances are therefore excellent opportunities for discerning the theological tendencies of each evangelist. One clue of what is going on here is that, while the evangelists often share the same narrative line through the passion and even the empty tomb, they part company in describing the resurrrection appearances. In fact, the original Gospel of Mark, which ends at 16:8, has no resurrection appearance at all. This is not to say, of course, that the evangelists' narratives of the appearances are of no great interest. Through them, the inspired Word of God instructs us more deeply concerning the ramifications of the resurrection.

The Empty Tomb

Besides the resurrection appearances, the other block of material which appears in the "resurrection chapter" of our Gospels involves the tradition about the empty tomb. Not long ago it was fashionable to dismiss the empty tomb tradition as a "late legend," since the tradition is not explicitly mentioned in the earliest Christain writings.

It is, however, firmly rooted in all four Gospels, John as well as the Synoptics. Today there would be more readiness on the part of many scholars to acknowledge that behind the empty tomb stories in our Gospels lies an early tradition. But this tradition seems to have developed independently of the story of the appearances to Cephas, the Twelve, and others. From the beginning, the empty tomb tradition involved at least Mary Magdalene, and perhaps some other women as well. Obviously, the tradition was tied to Jerusalem, and some commentators suggest that our present story arises out of a cultic celebration, a sort of liturgy held perhaps annually by Christians at the empty tomb. Be that as it may, it was only secondarily, but before the composition of our Gospels, that the two traditions of the empty tomb and the resurrection appearances were welded together to form the "Easter story," as we know it today.

Moving now to Matthew's recycling of the resurrection traditions, we see that the two ends of chapter 28 represent the two major strands of resurrection traditions: the empty tomb (28:1–8) and the appearance of the risen Jesus (28:16–20). In between we have two special Matthean traditions: the appearance to the women as they run from the tomb (28:9–10) and the bribing of the guard (28:11–15).

The Resurrection
(Also Mark 16.1–10; Luke 24.1–12; John 20.1–10)

28 After the Sabbath, as Sunday morning was dawning, Mary Magdalene and the other Mary went to look at the grave. ²Suddenly there was a strong earthquake; an angel of the Lord came down from heaven, rolled the stone away, and sat on it. ³His appearance was like lightning and his clothes were white as snow. ⁴The guards were so afraid that they trembled and became like dead men.

⁵The angel spoke to the women. "You must not be afraid," he said. "I know you are looking for Jesus who was nailed to the cross. ⁶He is not here; he has risen, just as he said. Come here and see the place where he lay. ⁷Quickly, now, go and tell his disciples: 'He has been raised from death, and now he is going to Galilee ahead of you; there you will see him!' Re-

member what I have told you." ⁸So they left the grave in a hurry, afraid and yet filled with joy, and ran to tell his disciples.

⁹Suddenly Jesus met them and said, "Peace be with you." They came up to him, took hold of his feet, and worshiped him. ¹⁰"Do not be afraid," Jesus said to them. "Go and tell my brothers to go to Galilee, and there they will see me."

¹¹While the women went on their way, some of the soldiers guarding the grave went back to the city and told the chief priests everything that had happened. ¹²The chief priests met with the elders and made their plan; they gave a large sum of money to the soldiers ¹³and said: "You are to say that his disciples came during the night and stole his body while you were asleep. ¹⁴And if the Governor should hear of this, we will convince him, and you will have nothing to worry about." ¹⁵The guards took the money and did what they were told to do. To this very day that is the report spread around by the Jews.

¹⁶The eleven disciples went to the hill in Galilee where Jesus had told them to go. ¹⁷When they saw him they worshiped him, even though some of them doubted. ¹⁸Jesus drew near and said to them: "I have been given all authority in heaven and on earth. ¹⁹Go, then, to all peoples everywhere and make them my disciples: baptize them in the name of the Father and of the Son and of the Holy Spirit, ²⁰and teach them to obey everything I have commanded you. And remember! I will be with you always, to the end of the age."

Easter Sunday

In the empty tomb story, Matthew has only two women, while Mark has three. While Mark gives as the reason for the visit the desire to anoint Jesus' body, Matthew simply says that the women came to see the tomb, as was previously mentioned in accord with the customs of mourning.

Matthew has colored the death of Jesus on the cross with apocalyptic hues (earthquake, the raising of the dead, their appearances in the holy city Jerusalem). He now undertakes the same apocalyptic coloring of the empty tomb tradition. This presented some difficulties, since, as we have seen, there seems to have been a generally understood, but unspoken, prohibition in early Christian tradition against portraying the resurrection of Jesus itself. Matthew takes some of the elements of Mark's account and recasts them to bring out his apocalyptic themes. Matthew also sees the death-resurrection as one event; thus the account of the opening of the tombs at the crucifixion overlaps with the resurrection story and the earthquake and is really the same event as the earthquake at Jesus' death. The characters portrayed at the resurrection scene mirror the responses of fear and faith. Unlike the guards at the cross, these guards are immobilized with fear. The angel (representing God's own action) dispels the fear of the women. "You must not be afraid." The angel proclaims the basic Easter message, which is meant to free the women and all believers from fear. The angel also orders the women to remind the disciples of Jesus' promise in 26:32. He adds that the disciples will see Jesus there.

Only Matthew, among the synoptic Gospels, has the scene of Jesus meeting the women as they return from the empty tomb (28:9–10). Yet 28:9–10 has a striking resemblance to a scene in John 20:14–18. Jesus' greeting is often translated as "hail," "greetings," or "peace." But the Greek verb used by Matthew literally means "rejoice." While Jesus' message to the women is essentially the same as the angel's, the incident has the purpose of making several important points. The risen Jesus is the same as the Jesus of the pre-resurrection. Matthew stresses this referring to him simply as Jesus with no other titles added. The women can touch him. He is physically real, not a dream.

■ *Reflection*

How would I describe the risen Jesus who is present in the Church today? Is he the same Jesus of the Gospels?

Reconciliation

Jesus refers to the disciples as "brothers." This would seem to indicate a reconciliation with those who had deserted Jesus at the time of his death. The fellowship is resumed in the new age of the kingdom. The promise of the Last Supper is fulfilled.

In 28:11–15 we see a number of sad ironies running throughout the story. The "cover story" invented for the guards makes them witnesses to an event that happened "while (they) were asleep." The Jewish leaders seek to solve their problems with money, just as they had when recruiting Judas. Further, they invent a falsehood to counter what they feared would be a deception on the part of the followers of Jesus. An added aspect here is that during most of his Gospel, Matthew—except when non-Jews are speaking—used the word "Israel" rather than "Jews." Now instead he himself speaks of "Jews." This may imply that the "Jews" have lost their claim to the status of "people of God." The Church is the new people of God.

The last section of the whole Gospel (28:16–20) is a miniature jewel of Matthew's theology. It has been called the key to the understanding of the whole Gospel. In a sense, one can understand this section only after one has worked one's way through the entire Gospel. And, on the other hand, after reading 28:16–20, one can go back and read the rest of Matthew's work with greater insight. We should read 28:16–20 with an appreciation of the change it proclaims in contrast to the situation presented throughout most of the Gospel. During his public ministry, Jesus restricted his mission in principle to the land and people of Israel (15:24) and laid the same restriction on his apostles (10:5–6). The mission to Israel naturally presumed adherence to the practice of circumcision and obedience to the Mosaic law. But between all this and 28:16–20 stands the yawning chasm of the death-resurrection, the turning of the ages. The appearance and mandate of the risen Jesus in 28:16–20 make clear what a change has been brought about in salvation history by the death-resurrection.

The Disciples Are Sent Forth

The whole of 28:16–20 can be conveniently divided into two major halves: the narrative in verses 16–18a and the sayings of Jesus in verses 18b–20. Let us discuss the narrative section first. This is the only time in Matthew's Gospel that we run into the precise phrase "the eleven disciples," a terse reminder of the role of Judas. Jesus of course began his earthly mission in "Galilee, and of the Gentiles!" (4:15). But in 4:15 the phrase carried more of the idea of a spiritually deprived, half-pagan land. Here it represents "all peoples," the object of the disciples mission.

Especially surprising to the reader is Matthew's statement in 28:17 that some or all the disciples (the Greek is not clear here) "doubted" or "hesitated." The Greek verb used here has been used elsewhere in Matthew to refer to personal hesitation and panic rather than theoretical doubts about doctrinal matters (see 14:31). The problem of "little faith" still remains. Perhaps there is a veiled message to members of Matthew's Church.

We move now to the three sayings of Jesus in verses 18b–20. Notice how the three sayings comprise the reporting of a past event (verse 18b), the issuing of a command for the present and future (verses 19–20a), and the making of a promise for the present and future (verse 20b). Strictly speaking, the Greek verb "was given" refers to a single event in the past. The event, of course, is the death-resurrection. Verse 18b seems to contain a reference to the scene involving "one like a Son of Man" in Daniel 7:13–14. Elsewhere in Matthew Jesus has used this passage from Daniel to describe his final coming at the end of time (see Matthew 24:30). A common representation of the resurrection in the early Church was Daniel in the lion's den.

At first glance, one is surprised by the "trinitarian" baptismal formula in Matthew 28:19. No doubt it represents the liturgical practice of Matthew's Church, not the practice of the earliest Christians (see Acts 2:38; 10:48). But the trinitarian formula is not without its preparation in Matthew's Gospel. Certainly we can see the reference to the baptism of Jesus, an event at which all three were present. Further, the formula implies that all three persons are equal. It is in the name of the Trinity that disciples enter the Church through baptism. Jesus then promises his continued presence with the Church "to the end of the age," an anticipation of the final coming of the kingdom promised throughout the Gospel of Matthew.

■ *Reflection*

How does Jesus' commission to the disciples apply to the Church today? How does it apply to me?

■ Discussion

1. Why does Matthew present the death and resurrection of Jesus as one event?
2. Why was the concept of the "empty tomb" so important to the members of Matthew's Church?
3. In Matthew's Gospel, how has Jesus been changed by the resurrection?
4. How does Jesus' final message to the disciples give us insight into what Matthew believed the Church ought to be?
5. Based on your reading of the entire Gospel, what do you think Matthew is trying to say about the meaning of discipleship?

■ *Prayer and Meditation*

"I passed on to you what I received, which is of the greatest importance: that Christ died for our sins, as written in the Scriptures; that he was buried and that he was raised to life three days later, as written in the Scriptures; that he appeared to Peter and then to all twelve apostles. That he appeared to more than five hundred of his followers at once, most of whom are still alive, although some have died. Then he appeared to James, and afterward to all the apostles. Last of all he appeared to me. . . ."

1 Corinthians 15:3–8

Bibliography _____

STUDY SESSION ONE

John P. Meier, *Matthew*. New Testament Message
Commentaries #3; Wilmington, DE: Michael Glazier,
Inc., 1980.

_____, *The Vision of Matthew*. New York, NY—Ramsey,
NJ—Toronto: Paulist, 1979.

Raymond E. Brown, *The Birth of the Messiah*. New York,
NY: Doubleday, 1977.

STUDY SESSION TWO

W.D. Davies, The Sermon on the Mount. New York,
NY—London: Cambridge University Press, 1966.

G. Barth, "Matthew's Understanding of the Law,"
in G. Bornkamm, G. Barth, H.J. Held, *Tradition and
Interpretation in Matthew*. Philadelphia, PA:
Westminster, 1976.

R. Banks, *Jesus and the Law in the Synoptic Tradition*.
New York, NY—London: Cambridge University Press,
1975.

John P. Meier, *Matthew*. Volume three in the New
Testament Message Series. Wilmington, DE: Michael
Glazier, Inc., 1980.

_____, *The Vision of Matthew*, 62–66, 222–262.

STUDY SESSION THREE

H.J. Held, "Matthew as Interpreter of the Miracle Stories." in G. Bornkamm, G. Barth, H.J. Held, *Tradition and Interpretation in Matthew*. Philadelphia, PA: Westminster, 1976.

B. Gerhardsson, *The Mighty Acts of Jesus According to Matthew*. Lund: Gleerup, 1979.

J.P. Meier, *Matthew*, 79–101.

_____, *The Vision of Matthew*, 67–73.

STUDY SESSION FOUR

J. Jeremias, *The Parables of Jesus*. New York, NY: Charles Scribner's Sons, 1972.

C. Carlston, *The Parables of the Triple Tradition*. Philadelphia, PA: Fortress Press, 1975.

J.D. Kingsbury, *The Parables of Jesus in Matthew 13*. Richmond, VA: Knox, 1969.

J.P. Meier, *Matthew*, 141–154.

_____, *The Vision of Matthew*, 89–93.

STUDY SESSION FIVE

D. Senior, *The Passion Narrative According to Matthew*. Louvain: Leuven University Press, 1975.

J.P. Meier, *Matthew*, 179–207.

STUDY SESSION SIX

R. Fuller, *The Formation of the Resurrection Narratives*. New York, NY: Macmillan, 1971.

R. Brown, *The Virginal Conception and Bodily Resurrection of Jesus*. New York, NY—Ramsey, NJ—Toronto: Paulist, 1973.

X. Leon-Dufour, *Resurrection and the Message of Easter*. London: Chapman, 1974.

N. Perrin, *The Resurrection According to Matthew, Mark and Luke*. Philadelphia, PA: Fortress Press, 1977.

J.P. Meier, *Matthew*, 359–374.

_____, *The Vision of Matthew*, 207–215.

Matthew

An Access Guide
for Scripture Study

Leader's Manual

Edmund F. Gordon

The content of this program
reflects the goals of *Sharing
the Light of Faith* (NCD)

William H. Sadlier, Inc.

New York   Chicago   Los Angeles

Nihil Obstat:
Joseph R. McMahon
Censor Deputatus

Imprimatur:
Paul J. Taggart
Vicar General
Diocese of Wilmington
November 22, 1982

Library of Congress Catalog Card Number: 82-61456
International Standard Book Number: 0-8215-5935-4
  23456789/987654

Published by
William H. Sadlier, Inc.
11 Park Place
New York, New York 10007

Contents

Preface

The *Access Guide* series is one response to the directive of the Fathers of Vatican II to provide "easy access to the Scriptures." Since Vatican II, efforts have been made to bring the people and the Scriptures together: the new *Lectionary* has been revised to present most of the Scriptures during a three-year liturgical cycle; new translations of the Scriptures are available; a scriptural orientation is now included in most religious education materials. These and other endeavors by educators, liturgists, and publishers have all been aimed at bringing the Word of God closer to his people. The charismatic movement has also given impetus to the renewed interest in the Scriptures.

Today, more and more Catholics are asking for materials on the Scriptures. They are finding that when they go directly to the text of the Scriptures, they can run into difficulties understanding what meaning the Gospel authors intended to convey. It is true that the Scriptures are the Word of God for us, but they are also works originally written in a foreign language, in an ancient time, for a different culture.

This series has been prepared to aid Christians who want to study the Gospels more thoroughly. It is a first-step study which presents each Gospel in light of sound biblical scholarship. The *Access Guides* may be used by an individual by himself or herself, but are especially designed for study groups working together. When Christians come together to break open and share the Word of God, a special dimension is added.

Purpose of the Study Group

There are two main purposes for the study group. First, the group studies a Gospel in its entirety to attempt to find out what the author-evangelist intended. In this way, the unique insights of the evangelist enrich the image of Jesus for each participant.

A second purpose of the study group is to know better the Jesus of the Gospels and thereby to deepen each participant's relationship with Jesus. This experience could lead to a life deeper in faith and enriched forms of prayer.

Each session has a double emphasis. On one level, the emphasis is on understanding and discussing the author's commentary and the scriptural text itself. On another level, the focus is on aspects of the Scriptures as they relate to our lives today.

The suggested discussion questions and activities are designed for a session approximately two hours long. This includes a break.

The Group Leader

The group leader is not expected to be a biblical scholar or a trained theologian. The primary function of the leader is to facilitate study activity within the group. This role includes providing discussion questions which would be of interest to your group in particular, keeping the discussion from wandering too far afield, and insuring that everyone is included in the conversations.

The leader is also responsible to make sure there is an opportunity for prayer during each session, that refreshments are provided for the group, and that participants are notified if there is any change in schedule. After the first session, the leader may ask the participants to create the prayer experiences and to bring refreshments.

While it has been stated that the group leader need not be a biblical theologian or scholar, the leader should be in touch with someone (priest, director of religious education, professor) who is conversant with Scripture study. This resource person should be able to provide answers to specific questions or problems which may arise in the group and which cannot be answered by the group leader or any member of the group.

Study Session One ———————— Matthew 1:1—4:22

Opening Exercise

Have the participants introduce themselves to one another. Then invite each person to give some autobiographical material and say a few words about why he or she wants to study Scripture and what he or she hopes to get out of the course. You might have the participants complete statements such as:

For me, the Church is ———— *because...*
The way to live a moral life is ———— *because...*

Introduction

The group leader gives out the guides for the study group and a schedule or calendar of the time and place for each of the sessions. Prepare, in advance, to give an overview of the main points covered in the preface and the general introduction. Assign these two sections as required reading before the next meeting of the study group. Encourage participants to write out any reactions and/or insights they may have in regard to this information for possible sharing within the group. Discuss the outline of the Gospel as presented in the thumbnail sketch, and explain briefly the rationale behind the divisions, session for session.

Explain that the Scripture in this session covers the infancy stories about Jesus, Jesus' baptism by John, the beginning of Jesus' public ministry, and the call of the first disciples.

Reading

Ask the participants to read the Scripture and commentary for Study Session One. Allow about 15 minutes for the reading. When the reading is completed, find out if there are passages in the Scripture or the commentary which anyone found difficult to understand. Questions which cannot be answered within the group should be referred to the resource person.

Reflection and Discussion

- Explain that in the introduction to this session, the commentator states that the infancy narrative in Matthew's Gospel anticipates many themes that will be taken up in the narrative of the death and resurrection of Jesus. Have the group find examples of this anticipation.

Break

- Invite the group to share responses to question number 4 (under "Discussion" in the study guide) on the escape to Egypt, the killing of the children, freedom from slavery, and so forth.
- Refer to the commentary which explains that for Matthew, repentance is a change of heart and mind, spilling over into changed behavior. Ask: *What role should repentance have in your life today?*
- The commentator states that Matthew and Luke have different ideas about the original hometown of Joseph and Mary. Ask: *Why do you think the early Church saw no need to correct apparent discrepancies in the Gospel accounts?*
- If time remains, share responses to some questions for "Reflection" and "Discussion."

Assignment

Before the next meeting of the group, have the participants read the introductory material, as well as the Scripture and commentary for Study Session Two.

Study
Session
Two _____ Matthew 5:1—7:29

Introduction

Explain that the Scripture for this session focuses on the Sermon on the Mount. Matthew has constructed this great teaching on the Christian life. The Sermon reflects Matthew's understanding that a totally new age has dawned. The kingdom of heaven (or of God, as in some translations of Matthew) had begun in Jesus. The Sermon on the Mount contains the new law for the new time. It is a law beyond the legalism which had eroded and distorted the Mosaic law. It is, rather, a law of the spirit, a law seemingly impossible for fallen humankind, but a law attainable for humankind now redeemed by the blood of the Lord.

Opening Exercise

Share what you have learned from your resource person pertaining to the questions and problems from Study Session One. Ask the participants to relate any questions or problems they may have had understanding the assigned reading for this session. Write down any questions that are too technical or advanced for the group to answer. During the coming week, contact your resource person on these questions.

Reflection and Discussion

- Referring to the Beatitudes (Matthew 5:3—12), the commentator tells us "that only those who have heard and believed this happy good news are capable of hearing and acting on Jesus' "demands." Using Jesus' descriptions of those who are capable of being truly happy, discuss: *Why are those who know they are spiritually poor, (those who mourn, the pure in heart, and so forth) open to the good news of Jesus? more capable of attaining true happiness?*

Break

- Divide the participants into five subgroups. Assign to each subgroup one of the 'antitheses' found in the Sermon on the Mount: 5:21–26; 5:27–32; 5:33–37; 5:38–42; 5:43–48. Have each group reread the assigned Scripture passage and discuss it in light of these questions: *What action is Jesus calling us to? What would be necessary for Christians today to live in the way Jesus commands? Are these commands ideal, realizable, or unrealistic for the "ordinary" Christian? What would be the result if a person tried to live up to these commands? If the institutional Church as a whole tried? How should we deal—how do we deal—with persons who fail to live up to these commands?*

- Allow about 10–15 minutes for discussion in subgroups. When time is up have each subgroup share their discussion outcomes with the entire group. Invite all participants to comment, question, and share their insights. Then ask: *Of the "antitheses" found in the Gospel of Matthew, which one seems most demanding? Why? In what ways does the Sermon on the Mount point out that a follower of Jesus is called beyond literal observance of the law to an attitudinal change of heart?*

- If time remains, share responses to some questions for "Reflection" and "Discussion."

Assignment

Before the next meeting of the group, have the participants read the Scripture and the commentary for Study Session Three.

Study Session Three —————— Matthew 8:1—12:50

Introduction

Explain that the Scripture for this session encompasses five chapters of the Gospel of Matthew. We find Matthew gathering the miracles together and presenting Jesus as healer and teacher. Like most of Matthew's Gospel, the messages conveyed by the miracles speak on several levels. They tell us about Jesus of Nazareth; they speak also to Matthew's audience, to their concerns and questions; finally they speak to us about what the Church is and what being a follower of Jesus means.

Opening Exercise

Share what you have learned from your resource person pertaining to questions and problems from Study Session Two. Then ask if the participants have any questions or problems about the assigned reading for this session.

Reflection and Discussion

- State that the first three miracles of the reading (8:1—17) involve a leper, a gentile (Roman officer), and a woman. As the commentator points out, these persons were all "outcasts of society." Ask: *What significance would these "outcasts" have for Matthew's audience? What do they tell us about Jesus' own ministry?*
- State that Jesus says: "Go and find out what is meant by the scripture that says: 'It is kindness that I want, not animal sacrifices.' I have not come to call respectable people, but outcasts" (9:13). Discuss: *What examples in this section of Matthew's Gospel show that Jesus lived by this saying? How does Jesus*

show the Father to be a merciful God?

- Explain that Matthew chapter 10 is an account of Jesus' instruction to his chosen Twelve. Matthew shapes this account to speak also to his audience. Ask: *From this account can you describe some of the problems facing the Christian community immediately addressed by Matthew?*
- Explain that in Matthew 9:36 we read: "As he [Jesus] saw the crowds, his heart was filled with pity for them, because they were worried and helpless, like sheep without a shepherd." Read Ezekiel 34:1–16 aloud to the group. Discuss various ways in which Ezekiel's image shines through in Matthew's Jesus.
- Compare Mark 4:35–41 (Jesus Calms a Storm) with Matthew 8:23–27. Then ask: *What changes does Matthew make in the story? What effect do these changes have?*

Break

- Have the participants reread Mattthew 11:16–19. Ask: *How does this passage reflect our Christian attitude toward life and living* (that is, neither too much asceticism nor too much enjoyment, but rather just middle-of-the-road)? *Do you think Jesus was a joyful person?*
- Refer to the commentary which notes that when Jesus touched the leper to cure him, he (Jesus) became ritually unclean and therefore was barred from participating in religious activities. Ask: *Who are the unclean, the outcasts of today's society? Is the Christian attitude today one of reaching out to and touching these lepers? What do you think the attitude of many Christians would be if the Church deeply and seriously intensified and expanded its ministries to today's outcasts?*
- If time remains, share responses to some questions for "Reflection" and "Discussion."

Assignment

Before the next meeting of the group, have the participants read the Scripture and the commentary for Study Session Four.

Study
Session
Four _____ Matthew 13:1—19:30

Introduction

Explain that the Scripture for this session introduces us to the parables of Jesus. The Gospel of Matthew expands the number of parables contributed by Mark. Moreover, we are able to see clearly in Matthew how the evangelist and the early Church adapted the parables to meet their own catechetical and apologetical needs. Then the Scripture reveals how Jesus and the Jewish leaders grow further apart. Hostility increases, and Jesus predicts his suffering and death to the disciples. At the same time, Jesus continues—one could almost say he presses hard—to deepen his disciples' understanding of who he is and what his message is.

Opening Exercise

Share what you have learned from your resource person pertaining to questions and problems from Study Session Three. Then ask if the participants have any questions or problems regarding the assigned reading for this session.

Reflection and Discussion

• Explain how the commentary states that as we read these parables, we must be aware of three different possible levels of meaning: the meaning the historical Jesus intended; the reinterpretation given by the early Church; and the reinterpretation given by the evangelists.

Divide the participants into subgroups of at least two persons each. Assign each subgroup one of these parables in Matthew: 13:4–9; 13:24–30; 13:31–32; 13:47–50. Each subgroup is to discuss its parable in light of the three levels of meaning and, based on their understanding, to suggest how:

—Jesus may possibly have used it in his ministry;

—the early Church in its situation may have adapted it;

—Matthew presented it in the totality in his Gospel.

- Compare Jesus' reply to the disciples' question about his use of parables in Matthew 13:16–17 with the interpretation in Mark 4:13–14. Where Mark has the disciples not understanding the parables, Matthew has Jesus complimenting them. Discuss how the reply in Matthew fits in with the evangelist's intentions and his interpretation of Jesus' message.
- In Matthew 16:13–20, Jesus confers a new name and title on Peter. Ask: *What is the reason* (Peter's declaration of faith!) *for Jesus' conferral? How does Matthew use the next passage (16:21–28) to temper Peter's promotion?* Have the group read and discuss 18:15–17. Ask: *In what ways does the Church still foster the attitude of fraternal correction in Christian life?*

Break

- Discuss the Scripture for this session in terms of the insights it gives us for dealing with the reality of Church as composed of both sinners and saints.
- Say that Jesus tells us to be childlike in our attitude toward the Father. Have participants reread 18:1–4 and 19:13–15. Then ask: *Is there a difference between childlike and childish? What are the "good" characteristics Jesus is encouraging?*
- Commenting on the story of the Canaanite woman (15:21–28), explain that Jesus thus destroys one of the great barriers separating Jews and gentiles (non-Jews). Ask: *Does our Church build barriers against other religious groups? If so, what are some of these barriers? Should Jesus' actions and attitudes tell us something about ecumenical activities?*
- If time remains, share responses to some questions for "Reflection" and "Discussion."

Assignment

Before the next meeting of the group, have the participants read the Scripture and commentary for Study Session Five.

Study
Session
Five _____ Matthew 20:1—27:66

Introduction

Explain that in the Scripture for this session, Jesus leads his disciples up to Jerusalem. On the way he continues to teach them about their duties and about what it means to live in the end times. In Jerusalem, Jesus confronts the authorities for the last time. This section takes us through the passion, death, and burial of Jesus.

Opening Exercise

Share what you have learned from your resource person pertaining to questions and problems from Study Session Four. Then follow the usual procedure for dealing with problems or questions raised in regard to the assigned reading for this session.

Reflection and Discussion

- State that the parable of the workers in the vineyard (20:1—16) is an excellent vehicle for discussing the message of Jesus. Many people focus on the apparent "injustice" done to the "early" laborers. But just as the parable of the lost son (Luke 15:11—32) is not really about the son but the father, so this parable is not really about the laborers but the owner. It is a parable about the merciful Father. Discuss the meanings of the parable: *What does it tell about the kingdom of God? How could this parable speak to the issue of Israel's rejection of Jesus? What does it say about the nature of God the Father?*
- Say that the Gospel of Matthew relates how various religious leaders try to "trap" Jesus (22:17—46). Ask: *What are the*

questions they pose to Jesus? What does the level of questioning tell us about these leaders?

- Point out that Jesus states his case against the scribes and the Pharisees in 23:1–39. Discuss: *What specific charges does Jesus make against these leaders?*

Break

- Say that in discussing the passion narrative, the commentator states that we should notice how Matthew constantly heightens the dignity and majesty of Jesus, even in his suffering and death. Have the group discuss various examples of this technique in Matthew's passion story.
- Point out that both Peter and Judas failed Jesus. Ask: *What do their different responses tell us about sin and reconciliation?*
- Have the participants reread the Final Judgment (25:31–46). Discuss: *What are some ways in which we can apply the lesson of this passage not only to our individual Christian lives but also to life in the Church?*
- In Matthew's passion narrative, Jesus is always in control of the situation. Discuss: *How does this depiction of Jesus affect our understanding of his passion, death, and resurrection?*
- Have the participants discuss Matthew 27:51–54 as one of the most important statements of the Gospel on the meaning of Jesus' death.
- If time remains, share responses to some questions for "Reflection" and "Discussion."

Assignment

Before the next meeting of the group, have the participants read the Scripture and the commentary for Study Session Six .

Study
Session
Six_____ Matthew 27:57—66—28:1—20

Introduction

This session focuses on the resurrection narrative of Matthew. Since the resurrection is the central event of Christianity and because the Gospel was written not before but after the resurrection, it is important to recognize how resurrection faith permeates the whole Gospel. In a way, the resurrection could be the introduction to the Gospel, as well as its last chapter.

Opening Exercise

Share what you have learned from your resource person pertaining to questions and problems from Study Session Five. Discuss any questions participants may have in regard to their assigned reading of Scripture and commentary.

Reflection and Discussion

- Have the participants discuss the meaning of the commentator's statement: "No one saw the resurrection of Jesus."
- Some biblical scholars make the point that resurrection is different from resuscitation. Ask: *What is the distinction between the two? How does Matthew's account show this distinction?*
- Explain how the commentator suggests that there seemed to be an unspoken prohibition against portraying the resurrection itself in the early Church. Ask: *Why do you think there might have been such a prohibition? What images from the crucifixion does Matthew reuse in the resurrection story (28:2—7) to show the relationship between the two events? How does he see the relationship?*

- Discuss: According to the commentary, Matthew 28:16–20 has been called the key to understanding the whole Gospel.

Break

- State that the primary mission of the Church is to continue in word and deed to proclaim the risen Lord. In light of the study of this session, discuss how the members of the group understand this statement.
- In light of the entire study, discuss: *How does the Gospel according to Matthew reflect his conception of salvation history?*
- Have the group reread 28:18–20. Then ask: *How does Jesus' command "Go, then, to all peoples everywhere," apply to all Christians today? Does this mean we should all try to convert everyone else?*
- If time remains, share responses to some questions for "Reflection" and "Discussion."
- Ask participants to share some insights they have gained during the group sessions.

Discuss plans for continuing as a group with those participants who wish to study another of the Gospels using the *Access Guide* series.

Preface

"The Bible has an essential and indispensable role to play in Christian catechesis. As a source of inspiration and spiritual nourishment, the Bible ought to be a constant companion" (*Sharing the Light of Faith, National Catechetical Directory,* number 60a).

Every person involved in youth catechesis would agree with the sentiments of the authors of the *National Catechetical Directory.* Every person who has attempted to work with adolescents would also agree that interesting youth in Scripture study and reflection is no easy matter. Except for the few youths who exhibit a mature faith development, catechists and youth leaders often find that there is very little interest or inclination to study the Scriptures among teenagers. This is a contemporary reality which poses a challenge to the community of the Church. How do we help young people come to know and meet Jesus in the Gospel? How do we help young people relate the Gospel to their lives and relate their lives to the Gospel? Of course, these questions are not unique to adolescents, but when applied to teenagers in particular, they require creative and realistic responses.

Major Goals

Learning the stories. A central need for all Christians is to learn the stories of faith, particularly the Gospel stories which "enjoy preeminence as principal witness of the life and teachings of Jesus, the Incarnate Word" (*NCD,* 60ai). In this course the participants will be exposed to an entire Gospel (Matthew) and to all of the Gospel forms, for example, parable, miracle story, teachings, sayings, passion narrative, and resurrection stories. If young people are to come to know Jesus, they must learn the stories of faith.

Appreciating the meaning intended by the author. Our study of Scripture takes into account the world in which the Gospel is read today as well as the world in which the author wrote, and the audience for which he wrote. The commentary aims to help the reader appreciate the unique contribution of each evangelist and the evangelist's particular reason for writing his Gospel.

Learning how to relate the Gospel to one's own spiritual journey. The Gospel speaks to us today, but it does so through stories that are thousands of years old. How then can we attempt to bring the Gospel meanings into relationship with the lives of teenagers in the later part of the twentieth century? These sessions try to take one or two of the themes from a block of material being studied and create a dialogue between the Christian story and the young person's own story.

Developing a scriptural-based prayer experience. The Scriptures are both a treasury of prayers and a source of prayer. The psalms, for example, provide a treasury of prayers; as a person learns to read and reflect on the psalms, they become a source of prayer. Also, if a young person can even begin to meditate on the Scriptures, he or she will have a lifelong source of light and strength for the journey of faith.

The Group Leader

The group leader does not have to be a Scripture scholar in order to fulfill his or her role. The leader is a facilitator who helps and guides the group in its study of the Gospel. The leader should have a love and appreciation for the Scriptures, but he or she need not be a teacher in the traditional sense.

As envisioned, the group leader is a co-learner with the young persons in the group. He or she keeps the group on track, poses questions for discussion, and invites every member of the group to full participation. The leader tries to make sure that no one is left out and that no one dominates the group.

The leader should be in touch with someone (director of religious education, priest, professor) who is conversant with Scripture study and who can answer technical questions which are beyond the level of the group leader.

The Sessions

The sessions are set up for six time periods of approximately two hours each. Even in two-hour sessions it would be impossible to discuss all of the material covered in the commentary. Therefore, selective topics have been chosen for emphasis in the discussions.

With teenagers, participatory activities are often very helpful learning experiences. It is beyond the scope of this guide to provide the detailed activities. You may find good activities to use with this course available in your religious education or youth ministry office. You may also want to consider using a film or filmstrip as part of a session.

Reading

Plan to allow about 20 minutes at the beginning for the participants to read the materials. Experience dictates that few teenagers will complete an outside reading assignment. The few who do read the material may remember very little of it for a fruitful discussion. Since the purpose of this program is to help young people learn more about Scripture, and not to improve on their study habits, assume they have not read it.

Make a habit of eliciting comment from the group when the reading is completed. Ask the participants to share their problem passages with you and the group. Encourage them to help one another. You should not spend more than ten minutes on this. If questions arise beyond your ability to respond, plan to have an answer or explanation at the next meeting.

Study
Session
One _____ Matthew 1:1—4:22

Opening Exercise

Begin the session with this get-acquainted exercise. Have the participants introduce themselves to one another. Then give each participant a piece of paper and a pencil. Explain what a family (genealogy) tree is. Show the members how to draw it, starting with their own generation of siblings at the bottom of the paper. Give the group five minutes to fill in as many generations prior to their own as they can. Have each one then share some things about himself or herself and explaining his or her family tree. Make sure that each participant has opportunity to share and explain.

Introduction

The leader gives out the guides for the study group and explains the purpose of the course. Since we have assumed that the participants will do no outside reading, the leader introduces the Gospel of Matthew to the participants. Material for this presentation (no more than 10 minutes) should be taken from the introductory material (preface, general introduction, and thumbnail sketch).

Explain that the portion of Scripture for Study Session One covers the infancy narrative, Jesus' baptism, the beginning of his public ministry, and the calling of the first disciples.

Reading

Allow time for the participants to sit quietly and read the material for Study Session One. When the participants have completed the reading, find out if there are any passages in Scripture or commentary which they found difficult to understand. Encourage all participants to share insights and opinions about these difficulties. Questions which cannot be answered within the group should be referred to the resource person.

Break

Reflection and Discussion

- You might want to reinforce the idea that the Gospels are not biographies of Jesus as we know biographies, but rather that they are faith-documents written by believers for believers. Divide the participants into three subgroups. Explain that the commentator says that the first two chapters of Matthew can be summed up by using three questions. Have each subgroup take one question and find the answer from chapters 1 and 2 of Matthew. For example, subgroup one finds all the titles of Jesus. When the subgroups complete the task, read each of the questions and have the subgroup present their answers to the entire group.
- Point out that the commentator tells us that the Gospels do not agree on the place where Joseph and Mary came from. This is only one example of many discrepancies among the Gospels. Ask: *Why do you think that the early Church saw no need to reconcile these discrepancies? What does this fact tell us about the purpose of the Gospels?*
- Explain that one of the important themes in Matthew is that Jesus sums up in himself the great events of Israel's sacred history. Have participants cite and discuss examples of how Matthew sees Jesus as the new Moses and the new Exodus.
- If time remains, share responses to some questions for "Reflection" and "Discussion."

Study Session Two _____ Matthew 5:1—7:29

Introduction

The Scripture for this session takes us through the Sermon on the Mount. Jesus presents the law for the new era, for the new kingdom of God. He, like Moses, goes to a mountain; Moses received the law, but Jesus proclaims the law. Jesus calls his followers beyond the legal interpretation of the covenant to a new law of the spirit.

Opening Exercise

Share what you have learned from your resource person pertaining to questions and problems from Study Session One. Encourage a brief review of the Scripture covered in the previous session.

Ask the group to discuss these questions: *What kinds of persons do you think are most capable of hearing God, that is, are most receptive to God's acting in their lives? Give reasons for responses. What kinds of persons seem to be least able to hear God? Give reasons.* Have participants make a list of the characteristics that seem most likely to make a person receptive to hearing the good news of Jesus.

Reading

Allow time for the participants to sit quietly and read the Scripture and commentary for this session. Encourage them to share any questions or problems they have about the reading. Follow the suggested procedure for dealing with questions and problems beyond the scope of the group.

Break

Reflection and Discussion

- Point out that the commmentator tells us that the Beatitudes (5:3–11) contain a list of characteristics of persons who are capable of hearing Jesus' good news. Compare these characteristics with the list arrived at by the group in the opening exercise of this session. Are there many similarities? Discuss why people who know they are spiritually poor, who mourn, who are humble, and so forth, are open and able to hear the good news.

- Assign each of these antitheses to an individual or a subgroup depending on the size of the whole group: 5:21–26; 5:27–30; 5:31–32; 5:33–37; 5:38–42; 5:43–48. Give the following directions: *Examine the statement of Jesus assigned to you or your subgroup. What does Jesus call for in this statement? Is Jesus' demand realistic? Is it difficult? Do you think that Jesus means these laws to be taken literally? Do you think that the Church is trying to live by these laws today?*

- Have the group reread 6:5–15. Then ask: *What does Jesus teach about prayer? How can we apply his teaching to our own lives? Is Jesus saying that no one should pray in public?*

- Have the group reread 6:16–18. Then ask: *Are there values for us from fasting? How can fasting help a young person today?*

- If time remains, share responses to some questions for "Reflection" and "Discussion."

Study Session Three _____ Matthew 8:1—12:50

Introduction

Recall how in the Scripture for Study Session Two Matthew portrays Jesus as lawgiver for the new age, for the kingdom of God. In the Scripture for Session Three, Matthew presents Jesus as miracle worker. The wonders that accompany the ministry of Jesus and of his Church are signs of the presence of the kingdom of God. The Scripture for this session stresses also Jesus' teaching about what it means to be his disciple, his follower.

Opening Exercise

Share what you have learned from your resource person pertaining to questions and problems from Study Session Two. Encourage a brief review of the Scripture covered in the previous session.

Begin this session by asking if any members have ever experienced what they would consider a miracle or if any of them know someone else who has experienced a miracle. Ask: *What was the miracle? How did it come about? What were the results?*

Poll the group, using these questions: *How many believe in miracles? What do you "believers" mean by the word "miracle"? How many do not believe in miracles? What do you "nonbelievers" mean by "miracle"? Why do you believe or not believe in miracles?*

Explain that this session's Scripture contains a collection of miracle stories from the Gospel of Matthew. Ask the group to pay close attention to the structure of these miracle stories, for example, who approaches whom, the condition for the miracle, and so forth.

Reading

Allow time for the participants to sit quietly and read the Scripture and commentary for this session. Encourage them to share any questions or problems they have about the reading. Follow the suggested procedure for dealing with questions and problems beyond the scope of the group.

Break

Reflection and Discussion

- Explain that the first three miracles (in this session's Scripture text) are worked for those considered outcasts from the Jewish society of Jesus' day. Discuss: *What intention could Matthew have had in presenting these miracles first? How do they reinforce Matthew's intention to show how the mission of Jesus' Church is now universal?*
- Have the participants reread 8:23–27. Explain that an ancient image of the Church is "the bark (boat) of Peter." Discuss how this image contains a message for the Church of Matthew's time and for the Church of our time today.
- Review Matthew's understanding of salvation history:
  Phase One—Time before Jesus' coming (hope of Jews in promise of his coming)
  Phase Two—Time of Jesus (his ministry limited to Jews)
  Phase Three—Post-resurrection era (universal ministry).
  Then discuss: *How are these three phases seen in Jesus' missionary discourse (10:5–40)? What does this discourse tell us about Matthew's audience?* (Try to work backward from this Gospel passage to discover some of the trials and problems Matthew is addressing.) *What message does this discourse have for Christians today?*
- Have the group use 11:16–19 to explain that Jesus could not follow public opinion as the basis for his style of ministry. He seems almost frustrated by what people expect of a prophet, of the Great Prophet. Then discuss: *How can this passage be applied to our own understanding of Jesus' mission and message? Do we expect Jesus to challenge us, to make us uncomfortable? Or do we expect him to comfort us, to accept us as we are? How do we keep these two attitudes and aspects in healthy tension?*
- If time remains, share responses to some questions for "Reflection" and "Discussion."

Study
Session
Four _____ Matthew 13:1—19:30

Introduction

Explain that this session introduces us to the parables of Jesus. The parables are used by Matthew to show the everwidening gap between Jesus and his followers and the leaders of Israel. The parables were used by the early Church in its catechetical efforts and also in its confrontations with others outside the Church. Because parables have many interpretations, they are suited to exploring the mystery of God's kingdom. We also find in this section Peter's profession of faith in Jesus, the feeding stories, and the first predictions of the passion.

Opening Exercise

Share what you have learned from your resource person pertaining to questions and problems from Study Session Three. Encourage a brief review of the Scripture covered in the previous session.

Point out that among all the Christian churches, a distinctive feature of the Roman Catholic Church is the Petrine Office or the ministry of the pope. Begin by inviting the members of the group to share their understanding of the ministry and role of the pope in the Catholic community. Ask: *What roles does the pope have in the life of the community? How does he exercise his ministry? Would the Catholic community be different if there were no pope? What would the difference be? How important is the pope in the life of the Church?*

At the completion of this exercise explain that this session contains some of the Scriptural passages which the Church interprets as supportive of the Petrine Office. Ask the group to pay close attention to these passages.

Reading

Allow time for the participants to sit quietly and read the Scripture and commentary for this session. Encourage them to share any questions or problems they have about the reading. Follow the suggested procedure for dealing with questions and problems beyond the scope of the group.

Break

Reflection and Discussion

- Review the three levels of meaning in the parables. Then proceed to divide the group into two subgroups. Assign each subgroup a parable from Matthew 13:4–9 or 13:24–30. Have each subgroup discuss the parable and try to see what possible meaning it could have had on the three levels: that is in the life of Jesus; in the early Church; for Matthew himself. Have each subgroup present its interpretations to the group at large. Finally, have the entire group discuss what meaning the parables might have for the Church today.
- Have the group reread Matthew 16:13–28. Ask: *What effect does Matthew achieve by placing the prediction of the passion immediately after Peter's declaration? What does this passage tell us about true leadership and discipleship?*
- In Matthew 18:1–5, Jesus speaks about receiving the kingdom of God like a child. Discuss: *Is there a difference between childlike and childish? What qualities of a child are true disciples of Jesus to maintain?*
- If time remains, share responses to some questions for "Reflection" and "Discussion."

Study
Session
Five_____ Matthew 20:1—27:66

Introduction

Explain that in the Scripture for this session Jesus leads his disciples to Jerusalem. On the way he continues to instruct them on the meaning of discipleship and the mystery of the kingdom of God. However, it is finally by his own passion, death, and resurrection that Jesus shows the full meaning and gives full meaning to all of his life, his mission, his message.

Opening Exercise

Share what you have learned from your resource person pertaining to questions and problems from Study Session Four. Encourage a brief review of the Scripture covered in the previous session.

Begin by reading Matthew 20:1—16. This parable (the workers in the vineyard) often provokes heated discussion because the natural identification is with the workers. But, like the story of the lost son (Luke 15:11—32), the focus should really be on the generosity of the vineyard owner, as it should be on the generous father of the prodigal son in that story. Allow the group to respond to the parable. Ask: *Is the vineyard owner just? What is justice? If we shift our focus from workers to owner, how does our perception of the parable change?*

Reading

Observe that in life "things are not always what they seem." Suggest that the group read this session's Scripture and commentary with that thought in mind. Encourage participants to share any questions or problems they have about the reading. Follow the suggested procedure for dealing with questions and problems beyond the scope of the group.

When the reading is completed, ask members of the group to share any examples they may have found which, like the parable of the laborers, take on a different meaning when viewed from a different perspective.

Break

Reflection and Discussion

- Divide the group into two subgroups. Assign each subgroup a parable, either Matthew 21:33—46 or 22:1—14. Have each subgroup discuss how the parable displays Matthew's concern to show that the Church's mission is now to go beyond Israel.
- Point out that in chapter 23 of Matthew's Gospel, Jesus attacks and condemns the scribes and the Pharisees. Ask: *What are Jesus' basic criticisms of these leaders?*
- Matthew 25:31—46 depicts the final judgment. Discuss: *What will be the criteria for judgment? What can we learn from this passage about the basic elements of living a Christian life? In light of this passage, what do you think the primary ministry of the Church ought to be?* Refer to the commentary which states that throughout the passion narrative, Matthew portrays Jesus as the one in control. Ask: *Can you find examples in Matthew's passion story in which he portrays Jesus in this way? How does this portrayal affect our appreciation of Jesus' passion and death?*
- Point out the commentary as stating that in Matthew 27:51—54 we have one of the most important statements of the Gospel on the meaning of Jesus' death. Have the group reread the Scripture passage and the corresponding commentary. Discuss the four events and their meanings.
- If time remains, share responses to some questions for "Reflection" and "Discussion."

Study Session Six _____ Matthew 27:57—28:20

Introduction

Explain that this session deals with the resurrection stories of Matthew. As we have mentioned throughout, all four Gospels are shot through with resurrection faith. They are biographies of faith. In a sense, the resurrection stories are the preface as well as the conclusion of the Gospel. The resurrection is the event through which the Father says in a unique, once-for-all way, "This is my beloved Son in whom I am well pleased." Yet, as Matthew shows us, the resurrection can never be separated from Jesus' life nor from his passion and death.

Opening Exercise

Share what you have learned from your resource person pertaining to questions and problems from Study Sesssion Five. Encourage a brief review of the Scripture covered in the previous session.

Say that Christians are first and foremost an Easter people. Then discuss what that means. Ask: *How do you understand this statement? In what ways does the Church continue to preach the resurrection? What are the practical implications for Christians to say that we are living in resurrection times?*

You might want to read and discuss 1 Corinthians 15:3—8 as an example of the importance the early Church attached to Jesus' post-resurrection appearances. Notice who is listed first. The listing of names was done carefully. Peter's primacy of place, as first witness to the resurrection, is evident.

Reading

Allow time for the participants to sit quietly and read the Scripture and commentary for this session. Encourage them to share any questions or problems they have about the reading. If there is to be another meeting of the study group, follow the suggested procedure for dealing with questions and problems beyond the scope of the group.

Break

Reflection and Discussion

- Point out that in his resurrection narrative (28:1–7) Matthew uses some of the same elements that he uses to describe Jesus' death. Ask: *What are some of those elements? How does this technique tie the resurrection to Jesus' death? What is Matthew here telling his audience?*
- Say that Matthew 28:16–20 is often referred to as the key to understanding Matthew's whole Gospel. Have everyone read this Scripture passage and then discuss how it explains and sums up the whole Gospel. Give specific examples.
- Say that in Matthew 28:8–10 Jesus appeared to the women as they left the tomb. They were able to touch Jesus. Ask: *What does this phenomenon tell us about the relationship between resurrection life and this life?*
- Explain that scholars make a distinction between resuscitation and resurrection. Have the group discuss this distinction. Ask: *How does the fact that no one witnessed the resurrection, but instead found the empty tomb, help show this distinction?*
- If time remains, share responses to some questions for "Reflection" and "Discussion."

- To conclude this final session, encourage participants to share:
  —personal insights about the Gospel of Matthew;
  —new insights gained into Jesus and his message;
  —new insights gained into the nature of the Church and the meaning of discipleship;
  —personal benefits derived from studying the Scriptures within the study group.

Discuss plans for continuing as a group with those participants who wish to study another of the Gospels using the *Access Guide series.*